CIVIL WAR VIGNETTES OF
ACADIANA

OTHER BOOKS BY MORRIS RAPHAEL

The Battle in the Bayou Country (5th printing)
Weeks Hall—The Master of the Shadows
The Weeks Hall Tapes
How do You Know When You're in Acadiana?
Mystic Bayou (out of print)
Murder on the Teche Queen (out of print)
Halo for a Devil
The Loup-Garou of Côte Gelêe (2nd printing)
Maria—Goddess of the Teche
A Gunboat Named Diana
My Natchez Years
Ti-Nute—The Angel of Devil's Pond
My Brazilian Years (An Amazing Adventure)

CIVIL WAR VIGNETTES OF ACADIANA

A Sesquicentennial Commemorative (1861-2011)

MORRIS RAPHAEL

Morris Raphael 3-11-2011

BORDER PRESS
SEWANEE, TENNESSEE 2011

Best Wishes to my friend Patrick — a fine newspaper reporter. Hope you enjoy the book. Morris

Library of Congress Control Number:
2011901171

ISBN 978-0-9843150-4-8

Illustrations by the author

for Diane

Preserving local history is a noble contribution to the present generation, and appreciated even more by future generations.

ACKNOWLEDGEMENTS

This is my 14th book and, for the 14th time, I heartily thank my dear wife Helen for her literate support and for providing me with an environment that any author would cherish. Frankly, I wouldn't dare venture writing a book if she were not close by to assist me during those agonizing moments when I'm stuck with a problem. She has been the wind in my sails for all of my writing accomplishments.

Publishing a book is a tough chore, and since I've grown old and somewhat decrepit, I promised myself not to get involved in another nightmare. But my good friend, Diane Moore, who has encouraged me in my writings for almost four decades, talked me into this one. Furthermore, with her journalistic expertise, she's led the way in getting this book published. She's the successful author of many books, and I regard her as being one of the best writers in the State of Louisiana. I proudly dedicate this book to her.

Our good friend and writer, Victoria Sullivan, has also contributed her valuable time and efforts to this work. She formatted the copy and illustrations in an attractive manner. Diane's grandson, Martin Romero, who is a landscape architect, contributed his cover designing technique. Diane, Vickie, and Martin make a fine production team – I thank them all.

I want to thank my good friend Roland Stansbury, who is director of the Young-Sanders Center in Franklin, for providing me with historical information whenever I needed it. I am also grateful to Will Chapman, publisher of *The Daily Iberian*, for his help and cooperation in my writing career. Many more deserve my thanks and gratitude. I sincerely hope the public enjoys the contents of this book.

FOREWORD

The book is a compilation of human-interest stories and historical accounts of the Civil War as it was fought in the bayou country of Louisiana, a part of Acadiana, where Yankees and Rebels roamed the countryside and fought it out in bloody encounters. The stories were extracted from The Official Records of the U.S. Government, regimental histories, works of several authors, diaries and letters of soldiers, and reminiscences of others.

Publication of this book coincides with the Sesquicentennial – the 150th anniversary of the American Civil War, which was declared on April 12, 1861.

I hope you enjoy reading these rare historical accounts of yesteryear.

Morris Raphael
7 January 2011

TABLE OF CONTENTS

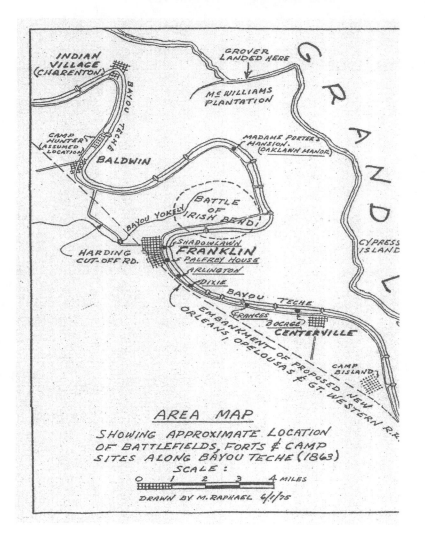

AREA MAP

SHOWING APPROXIMATE LOCATION
OF BATTLEFIELDS, FORTS & CAMP
SITES ALONG BAYOU TECHE (1863)
SCALE:
0   1   2   3   4 MILES

DRAWN BY M. RAPHAEL 6/1/75

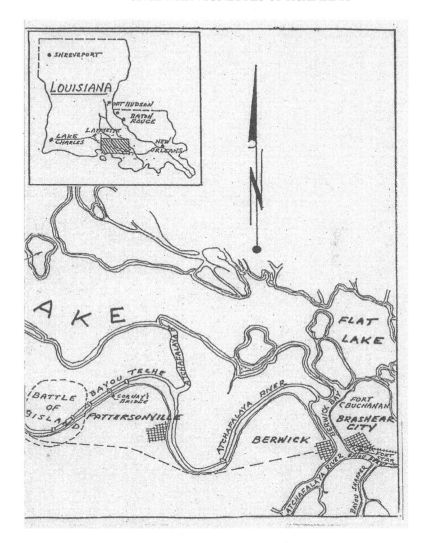

YANKEES TAKE OVER
FRANKLIN NEWSPAPER

The town of Franklin, Louisiana figured prominently during the War Between the States. It was there, on April 12 and 13, 1863, that Confederate General Richard Taylor, with a small army of 4,000 stalwarts, stopped the powerful Union juggernaut on two fronts. The Yankees, led by General Nathaniel Banks, with three brigades of about 18,000 men and powerful gunboats, finally overpowered the Rebels after a bloody struggle. However, the crafty Taylor escaped safely with his men to northwest Louisiana.

From all indications, the occupation of the Franklin area by the Yankees was an enjoyable venture for the invaders. Their scribes wrote about finding beautiful homes, gardens and plantations; delicious fruits and vegetables, and an abundance of lamb, pork, and beef. In essence, they felt they had fallen into a place that was extra special.

A letter written by Mattison, a Yankee scribe, to *The Boston Journal* on April 19, 1863, contained some interesting observations. He stated: "The town of Franklin is the shire town of St. Mary Parish, and is one of the neatest villages in the State. The Court House and jail are elegant brick buildings, and everyone here bears the signs of thrift and enterprise." He mentioned the town had two newspapers: *The Atchafalaya Register* and *The Planter's Banner*, and that "in the healthy times prior to the breaking out of this infernal and devastating rebellion, both were of ample fold and prosperous, but in these evil days of the South, they diminished in size and have literally 'gone to the wall.'"

Mattison pointed out that the newspapers were printed on the reverse side of rolls of wallpaper, and since printing paper had become a luxury, the craft could not afford $40 a ream for 500 sheets 25" x 32".

"Mr. I. O. White," he wrote, "was editor of *The Register* and a zealous Bell-and-Everett man, and also an avowed Unionist. He was regarded as untrustworthy by the Rebels, and so suffered much injustice in their hands. He was compelled to admit secession leaders into his paper in order to save his neck. When our troops occupied Franklin, he was one of the first to take the oath of allegiance. He is a native of the South and has enjoyed many emoluments from the people in the peaceful days of the old flag. He is bitter upon the leaders of the secession movement, which has brought so much disaster upon this fair country."

The Union scribe also reported that Daniel Dennett, "a rabid secessionist," formerly of Sacco, Maine, edited *The Planter's Banner* and when the Yankees occupied Franklin, "he skedaddled." Both newspaper offices were merged under the order of the Provost Marshal and Sergeant Charles G. Wing of the 22nd Maine, and a new Union paper was to be issued.

According to Mattison, the Mayor of Franklin was A. L. Tucker, a native of western New York who was a member of the seceding Louisiana State Legislature. He explained that many of the Franklin citizens were from the North and "more than one heart was led to rejoice that the full spell of secessionists' power has been broken and the starry flag again waves over the town."

General Taylor, however, lost no time in building a strong defense in the Mansfield area. When General Banks' troops attacked on April 8, 1864, they were clobbered, causing them to withdraw to Pleasant Hill where they were overpowered again in another bloody battle. The Rebels rejoiced in their victories.

Although Taylor was pleased, he was also saddened to lose his valiant General Alfred Mouton in the Mansfield engagement.[1]

---

[1] Mattison, a Yankee scribe, letter to the *Boston Journal*, July 19, 1863.

YANKEE SPY IN ACADIANA

A Spanish music man, who lived in St. Mary Parish, Louisiana, before the Civil War, became a spy for the Union Army. Benito Monfort, a resident of Cadiz, Spain, who immigrated to New Orleans in 1859, lived there for six months, and then settled at Indian Bend (Charenton), which is located along Bayou Teche, approximately four miles above Baldwin.

Monfort taught music as he made his rounds across the bayou country of Louisiana. One can surmise that he was a charming, outgoing individual who made a hit with the higher-ups in the region. When the War broke out, he fraternized with Confederate officials, and even General Henry H. Sibley, who eventually took charge of the Rebel forces at Fort Bisland near Centerville. This exemplified Monfort's magnetic and aggressive personality. Sibley, incidentally, was an alcoholic and probably made important revelations to the Spaniard.

In the Spring of 1863, when the War got into full swing, a Confederate militia law was being enacted whereby residents were required to enlist for at least a one-year period. This was definitely not to Monfort's liking, so he began making plans to leave for Havana, Cuba, a move, which he realized would require help from both the Confederate officials, who were entrenched in the Centerville/Franklin area, and the invading Union command, whose forces occupied the Brashear City/Berwick area. The two armies were located approximately twelve miles apart and were geared for battle.

Just before attempting his exit, Monfort made reconnaissances around the area, observing the military installations and manpower. He even visited Rebel officials, dined with Sibley, and they told him not to reveal anything he saw or heard to the Yankees. But, evidently, the Spaniard, thinking of saving his own hide, made notes just in case.

On February 21, 1863, Benito, under a flag of truce, entered the Union lines in the Berwick Bay area where he was immediately imprisoned and interrogated. According to a report by Union Lieutenant Pickney Allen to his commander General Godfrey Weitzel, Monfort revealed pertinent information, which included location of batteries, gunboat and troop locations, the number of troops, an organizational plan to beef up nearby Camp Pratt, and even presented them with a sketch showing the things he mentioned. Allen added that he believed what his prisoner said was true.

General Weitzel wrote Major N.P. Banks that he also believed what the Spaniard revealed was true. A report submitted by Brigadier General and Provost Marshal James Bowen to Lieutenant Colonel Richard Irwin was similar to that of Weitzel's. Bowen, stationed in the New Orleans area, stated, "I also submit a sketch drawn by the prisoner of the stations of troops of which he has personal cognizance, except at Fausse Point and Butte-a-la-Rose, and of those, from the information given him, he has no doubt the forces stated are at those points. I am inclined to place reliance in the statements he has made."

General Bowen added the following from Monfort's revelations: "The Hart, a medium-sized steamer, is at New Iberia; saw her on Monday at 3 p.m.; no one at work on her then; her machinery exposed to view (the front), protected by railroad iron; the country is destitute of provisions; troops will starve in three months." (The unfinished beefing up of the Gunboat Hart was cause for the Rebels to eventually scuttle the vessel as an added obstruction in the Bayou Teche to the Yankees' subsequent invasion by land and water).

Nothing more was learned about Monfort, but since he made his clandestine reports to the Yankee commanders, he, no doubt, was released to make his exit to Havana. Although the word "freedom" was music to the man's ears, he probably was later haunted by his betrayal of trust to the many friends he had made in the bayou country. He must have felt that if he returned, he would have been skinned alive.[2]

---

[2] *War of the Rebellion*, Records of the Union and Confederate Armies, Series 1, Vol. XV.

THE UNION ARMY MET FIRM RESISTANCE IN BAYOU COUNTRY ACTION

All was not peaches and cream for the mighty Federal forces under General Nathaniel Banks as they bulldozed their way through the fields and bayous of south Louisiana. They were confronted and tormented throughout the whole campaign. Confederate General Dick Taylor with his meager army exhibited firm resistance at Brashear City, Pattersonville, Bisland, Irish Bend, Vermilionville, Avery Island, Grand Coteau, as well as in other engagements.

On November 3, 1863, Union General Stephen Burbridge and his strong army, while encamped near Carencro, found themselves subjected to a hair-raising experience. Confederate General Tom Green led a surprise attack with cavalry, batteries, and some infantry as the Rebels inflicted heavy casualties on their enemy and confiscated much armament. This bloody onslaught was later known as the Battle of Bayou Bourbeau.

A Union scribe of the 83rd Ohio Volunteers related the severity of the attack in his diary: "The whole of the 67th Indiana was gone, except the Adjutant and Major, a few of the 6th Indiana was left, about a third of the 23rd

Wisconsin, a few of the 96th Ohio, and nearly all of our regiment and two battery pieces." In all, he stated, the 3rd Brigade lost 680 who were killed, wounded, and taken prisoners. Although the Confederate casualties were reported as 180, it is said that the count was much higher.

This devastating blow caused so much concern to the Union Command, it decided to direct its forces back to the Teche country as a precautionary measure. After the Brigade moved southwardly, a decision was made to proceed onward to New Iberia where it arrived and encamped on November 8, 1863. Immediately, a regiment of approximately 500 blacks was recruited and was called the 25th Louisiana of the *Corps d'Afrique*. They were identified with, and proud of, the bright red caps they wore. Their initial assignment was to construct fortifications in and around the town as protection from future attacks. Later, white citizens were forced to join in the work by a stern order from General Burbridge. According to a Union scribe, many resisted working side by side with blacks who, in some instances, were former slaves. The General advised his offices to use bayonets if necessary.

Since tents were scarce, the frequent rains caused much discomfort to members of the Brigade. This problem was quickly remedied as lumber of all kinds was secured and shelters were constructed. Even the constant drilling routine was eased to the point whereby the infantrymen found much relief and enjoyment for weeks to come.

However, on December 8, the Brigade was unexpectedly ordered to march and arrived at Franklin where a fort had been constructed and comfortable quarters arranged. These quarters were said to be some of the best they had found along the way. Later, the 83rd Ohio regiment was ordered to move fifteen miles to Patterson where the quartermaster accepted and issued meat, which was to be fed to the soldiers. The meat was said to be decayed, and the members of Company A were not going to stand for this, which caused quite a commotion in camp.

The soldiers secured a band, detailed a funeral escort, and with due solemnity, buried the offending material with a regular military funeral, closing with the regulation salute of guns fired over the grave. The entire proceeding was in full view of everyone and regimental officers watched it. Although the quartermaster did not like the mock funeral, since there was nothing offensive about the proceeding, the whole thing was passed off as a joke.

A letter by Ohio Yankee Isaac Jackson to his sister gives a very good description of the countryside. "This is very pleasant country and we have a very pleasant camp. It is all called the Teche Country, and I tell you it's nice, and the Bayou Teche is also nice. On either side are splendid plantations. The buildings are of the best and the country is rich. Orange, figs, bananas, lemons, and pecan nuts are abundant. And what is better than all, the people are loyal to a great degree. A great many took oaths on Banks' first arrival.

"We gathered oranges as we went along, by the sacks full, and pecan nuts as plenty as walnuts at home – but when we struck the prairie we found none of these. But still, we have fresh beef of the best quality. The soldiers generally are delighted with this country. Many say that after the war is over, they are coming down here to settle down." I found in my research that some Yankees did return to the bayou country. One such person was John T. White, a member of Company D, 83rd Ohio Infantry, who was well thought of in his regiment. He was discharged on February 20, 1864 to accept appointment as 2nd Lieutenant in the 76th Regiment, U.S. Colored Infantry (all officers were white).

White finally rose to the rank of Captain and, after being mustered out on December 31, 1865, he became a sugar farmer in south central Louisiana, and then moved to New Iberia where he had served as Provost Marshal during the War and became an insurance man and prominent citizen. In an 83rd Ohio regimental history published on September 12, 1912, White's address was listed in the "Semi-Centennial Roster" as Box 186, New Iberia, Louisiana. (I knew his grandson, Junius H. White, and we became good friends. He was Postmaster in this city from 1966-1972).

One Yankee scribe aboard the Steamer J. M. Brown described some of the things he saw on a cruise downstream from New Iberia to Brashear City. The steamer stopped at several landings along the way to take on sugar, one

of which was at the plantation of Madame
Porter. (Her luxurious mansion is now known
as Oaklawn Manor, and is the home of former
Governor Mike Foster. Madame Porter was
looked upon as a Yankee sympathizer and
probably made concessions to the Union
command). The scribe wrote: "She is said to
enjoy the advantage of a 'protection' and
manages to keep her 250 slaves. Not long
since, however," he continued, "she sent forty-
five of her best Negroes to Texas, to save
them, probably, as the men took a dose of
medicine. She is a kind mistress and has
erected a fine church for the use of her
chattels. She was much younger than her
husband, but married a fortune. She was a
beauty and is said now to be a splendid
looking woman. She has a house in
Washington, D.C. and one in Newport, Rhode
Island, at both of which places she has figured
as a rich and fashionable star. Her slaves
dread the return of the Rebels, fearing they all
will be sent to Texas; so, they are resolved to
follow our army when it leaves this Teche
country.

"But when is the army to leave? Supplies
largely in excess of their needs are rapidly

going to New Iberia; but is not the rainy season now so near at hand as to render an exhibition overland to Texas in a high degree of hazardous?"[3]

---

[3] This report was written on November 1, 1863. A few days later, as explained at the beginning of this article, the Yankees were clobbered at the Battle of Bourbeau.

GENERAL BANKS SLEPT AT BELMONT

It is an historic fact that Union General Nathaniel Banks and his staff made Belmont their headquarters when the Yankees occupied the New Iberia area during mid-April, 1863. Banks, who had replaced General Benjamin Butler in November of 1862 as Commander of the Gulf, including Texas, was successful in his invasion of the bayou country. His victories, which were not easily accomplished, included the gunboat battles along the Teche, the Battle of Bisland, and the Battle of Irish Bend. His troops were responsible for the destruction of the salt works at Avery Island.

According to a deposition claim filed February 28, 1883 by Bernard Suberbielle against the United States government, a large quantity of sugar and molasses were confiscated from the John F. Wyche plantation. Joseph C. Segura and Charles Bouligny, who were both sugar planters made statements confirming that Banks stayed at Belmont.

Segura, who lived approximately a mile from the Wyche plantation, testified that General Banks and his staff occupied Belmont for eight days, and that he understood from a

Mr. Dariet that the Yankees had taken 50 hogsheads of sugar and about 50 barrels of molasses (A hogshead of sugar weighed about 1200 pounds). He also indicated that rum was made on the plantation from corn and molasses.

Bouligny, who took charge of the Wyche plantation a few days before the arrival of the Federal forces, stated that he was the only person living on the place at the time. It may be well to mention here that during that period, Confederate Major John Fletcher Wyche, owner of the plantation, was serving in another section of the country. His wife, Mary, their four-year old son, James, and several slaves fled the premises prior to the Yankee takeover for fear of their lives and joined a wagon train headed for Texas. Bouligny testified that Union troops confiscated and hauled away huge amounts of sugar by means of four mule wagons. He mentioned that a Yankee also took his $300 horse.

According to Bouligny, the bayou country people living in the vicinity of the Wyche plantation destroyed all their skiffs in order to prevent the Yankees from crossing the bayou.

He stated that Federal stragglers took off the big doors of the sugar house and used them in their foraging operations. The door rafts, he explained, were used in crossing over to Mrs. de Spanet DeBlanc's place where chickens were stolen.

During the deposition, it was learned that the main segment of the invading Federal army camped on the Wyche premises one night and took off late the following morning in the direction of St. Martinville and Opelousas.

According to the Wyche family records, the Union troops removed the rosewood grand piano from the house, took the strings from it, and used it as a trough to feed and water their horses. Cabins were pulled down, fences were used for firewood, and some planking was removed from the home. Mary returned from Texas in 1865 and paid the back taxes on the plantation with gold they had earned from cotton crops in Texas. Mary and her family smuggled the gold back home by sewing gold pieces in their undergarments. Mary's son, James, was the father of James Wyche, Jr., the former owner of Belmont, who lived there with his wife and family until his death. His daughter, Mary Wyche Estes, now resides on the old plantation.

Much has been written about Belmont, and there's no record showing how far back in history the grounds were utilized by human beings. Arrows, pottery, and other artifacts indicate that the Attakapas Indians once lived on the property. Belmont is a part of the Spanish heritage in New Iberia. The original dwelling and plantation were established in 1765. The home itself was built for one of the Spanish commandants of the area.

Unfortunately, Belmont was destroyed by fire in 1947, and the home that exists today is a replica of the original dwelling. The old plantation bell, which was cast in 1859, is seen in a tower on the side of the house. This bell rang out on many Fourth of July celebrations that were held on the premises. It's amazing that after almost two and a quarter centuries, Belmont Plantation remains an outstanding operational, historical, and integral part of Acadiana.

THE MOSQUITO FLEET

It was June, 1863. Federal General
Nathaniel Banks had completed his conquest
of the Teche country and lower Red River
valley and was now engaged in the fierce siege
of Port Hudson. Confederate General "Dick"
Taylor, who had escaped to northwest
Louisiana with his small army, grasped the
opportunity to return to the bayou country.

Taylor immediately assigned two of his
crack brigadier generals, Alfred Mouton and
Thomas Green, the responsibility of
recapturing Brashear City (Morgan City). At
this site, large stores of equipment and
supplies were concentrated and were
protected by a Federal force, a wide body of
water known as Berwick Bay, a network of
lakes and bayous, and the gunboat
"Hollyhock."

Mouton and Green, with headquarters near
Pattersonville (Patterson), formulated a secret
plan and began collecting all the small craft,
such as skiffs, bateaux, dugouts, flats, and
"sugar-coolers," that they could locate in the
area.

This strange activity aroused the curiosity
and enthusiasm of the soldiers, and when
Green asked for 250 volunteers, more than
300 men from Texas and Louisiana

companies responded. Major Sherod Hunter of Baylor's Texas Regiment was placed in command of the 53-unit fleet, the largest boat being the "Tom Green," which was to carry fifteen men. Most of the vessels were sugar-coolers. These were long, coffin-like boxes used as syrup receptacles on sugar plantations. The sugar-coolers were improvised to accommodate one or two persons.

The unique armada began its strange mission at sunset on June 22, and the units traveled in pairs up the Atchafalaya, into and across Grand Lake, then eastward through timber passes, and across Flat Lake and Lake Palourde. The plan was that General Green set up a battery at Berwick, and at about dawn to fire across the Bay and draw the attention of the Federal forces at Brashear. In the meantime, the mosquito fleet was to launch a surprise attack at the rear of the city.

Before reaching the shoreline, the entire flotilla was halted, and the oarsmen were directed to muffle their oars with moss so that the sneak attack would be conducted as quietly as possible. The crew landed just before daybreak, but over 50 members of the fleet were lost because of darkness and an inability of some to navigate in swampy waters. While the invading force waded, waist deep, through the swampy terrain, soldiers began to hear the exchange of gunfire between Green's artillery and the Union defenders. The commander of the gunboat chose to back out of the action and retreated downstream to safety.

However, while Hunter's crew was approaching the fortification, there was hesitation in the ranks. The men were afraid they would fall into a trap and would be wiped out by Federal rifle fire and bayonets.

Major Hunter grouped his men and warned them: "We may all be shot." He continued, "Not one of us may get back to the brigade; but gentlemen, we'd better just fall down in our tracks rather than go back disgraced and have old Tom Green tell us so."

These words seemed to rally the southerners, and they began screaming and charging in the direction of the camps. The Federal troops were utterly taken by surprise. Although they tried to halt the advance of the charged-up Rebels, there was mass confusion in the camp. By 10 a.m., the fighting had

ended, and the garrison surrendered to
Hunter.

According to Hunter, his losses were very
light – three were killed and 18 wounded. He
claimed that 46 Yanks were killed, 40
wounded, and 1300 prisoners captured –
most of whom were convalescents. He
reported that 11 heavy artillery guns, 250
rifles, 2000 blacks, over 200 wagons,
hundreds of tents, and a huge quantity of
quartermaster, commissary, and ordinance
stores had been confiscated.

The triumphant Rebels took over the
garrison and celebrated by eating and
drinking to their hearts' content. Taking
Brashear City was an important victory for
Taylor, who realized an abundance of supplies
for the first time since his arrival in the Trans-
Mississippi Department.[4]

---

[4] Theo Noel, "A Campaign from Santa Fe to the
Mississippi": Lt. A.J. Duganne, 76th New York; General
Richard Taylor's, *Destruction and Reconstruction*; Morris
Raphael, *The Battle in the Bayou Country.*

THE ENIGMA AT IRISH BEND

In the Spring of 1863, Union General Nathaniel Banks began an all-out offensive to capture the Teche country of Louisiana. He set out from his base at Brashear City (now Morgan City) with three divisions numbering around 18,000 men. Occupying the Franklin area were the forces of Confederate General Richard Taylor. Although Taylor's small army did not exceed 4,000, most of his men were well entrenched behind earthworks at Fort Bisland, which was located abut 12 miles east of Franklin.

Banks ordered two divisions to attack Taylor's front at Bisland, while the remaining division under the command of General Cuvier Grover, was to land secretly behind Franklin, with plans to trap General Taylor, all his forces, equipment and provisions.

Grover's flotilla of four gunboats, three transports, tugs and flatboats, carrying a force of approximately 8000 men, made its way quietly through Grand Lake. When Taylor's intelligence reported an attempted landing behind his lines, he immediately dispatched a cavalry regiment and an artillery detail to ward off the attack.

But, apparently, landing was not a big problem for the Federals as the heavy guns of the gunboats raked the shoreline of Indian Bend (near Charenton), routing the small band of Confederate defenders and clearing the way for the Union invasion. Grover's division began landing about noon, April 13, at a point approximately seven miles northwest of Franklin. Before nightfall, the Union forces had penetrated about four miles toward Franklin and planned to bivouac in the vicinity of Madame Porter's mansion (now known as Oaklawn Manor).

Madame Porter was heralded as the proprietress of one of the richest plantations in the South. She owned several square miles of fertile farmlands, a large sugar mill and over 400 slaves. Her beautiful home located on the south bank of Bayou Teche stood about a half mile from the road and was placed under immediate protection by a detail of the 52nd Massachusetts Infantry Regiment.

The reader is asked, at this point, to picture the Teche Country as being one long, narrow, winding ridge extending in an eastwardly and westwardly direction. In the center of this ridge flows the Bayou Teche, with roads on both sides. To the north are Grand Lake and the rest of the Atchafalaya Basin. On the south are peninsulas, marshes, bays, and the Gulf of Mexico. North of Franklin, the Teche forms a sort of horseshoe. Located near the curved end of the horseshoe is Madame Porter's mansion. The east leg extends in the direction of Franklin, while the other leads to Baldwin. It may be well to mention here that Alexander Porter, who was a U.S. Senator, built the mansion in 1838 and purchased thousands of acres of land on both sides of the Teche. Porter and a few other settlers there, who were

47

Irishmen and steamboat captains, probably referred to the curve around Porter's plantation as Irishmen's Bend. Later, the area took on the abbreviated moniker of Irish Bend.

General Grover was pondering his next move as he sat astride his horse near a road intersection. Suddenly, a lank, grizzled soldier from Company "H" (52nd Massachusetts Regiment), carrying a musket on his shoulder, appeared with the queenly Madame Porter. She was described as a beautiful woman in her late forties who was bareheaded and elegantly dressed.

She stopped at the stirrups of General Grover and began pleading for the life of her son, who had just been taken prisoner.

"Please let him go, General," she begged. "The poor boy is quite innocent." She continued, "Please let him go, General. He is all I have." She repeated this over and over.

The General never uttered a word. He appeared not to be listening. The son, a tall, fierce-looking young man, of about 19 or 20 years of age, stood close by, under guard.

Presently, the same grizzled soldier escorted the disappointed lady back to her home.

Early the next morning, Grover pressed his forces toward Franklin. In the meantime, Taylor had pulled about 1200 of his troops from his entrenched position east of Franklin and posted them around a sugar cane field in the Irish Bend area. Some of the men were hidden in the woods, some in canebrakes, and others were behind fences. The Rebel gunboat "Diana" was also poised in the bayou behind the lines.

When Grover's regiments appeared across the open field, the Battle of Irish Bend commenced. A vicious Confederate attack caught the Union invaders by surprise and stopped them in their tracks. After experiencing heavy casualties, several of Grover's regiments were forced to retreat out of range of the Confederate gunfire.

But later in the day, Grover accumulated his superior force and re-activated his attack. By this time, however, Taylor had vacated his position, scuttled the Diana, and had withdrawn his forces from Bisland where they had made a heroic stand in spite of overwhelming odds.

Taylor's troops and wagon trains from both fronts were funneled into Franklin, simultaneously, and directed down Iberia Street and across the Harding property toward Baldwin, burning the Yokely Bridge as they sped to safety. This route was known as the "Cut-Off Road."

When the Union forces ran into each other at Franklin, they were chagrined to learn that Taylor and company had cleverly outmaneuvered them.

Although a desperate attempt was made to catch up with Taylor, the invaders were frustrated even more to learn that the bridge at Bayou Yokely has been destroyed. This delay gave Taylor all the room he needed. He, his men, and equipment were now well out of the grips of the Federal vise.

According to Union diaries and regimental histories, many of the officers and men felt that Grover had goofed at Irish Bend. There were insinuations that Grover, after landing, should have directed his troops to Baldwin where he could have bottled up Taylor's forces. It was later rumored in the Franklin area that Madame Porter was a Yankee sympathizer, that she entertained Union officers, and that she tried to persuade Grover to take the Baldwin leg of "the horseshoe."

Adding weight to this rumor was the fact that her mansion was not pillaged or burned, was constantly protected by Union troops, and her plantation was left fairly intact. Then, too, there is documented evidence from Homer Sprague's "History of the 13th Regiment of Connecticut Volunteers" relating that Madame Porter's son was released not long after he had been captured.

The late John Caffery, who was a Franklin sugar planter and historian, mentioned the Porter-Grover rumor in an article that was published in 1959. Caffery wrote that when Grover was questioned about Madame Porter's attempt to direct him to Baldwin, he denied that any such conversation had ever taken place.

However, the rumors that Madame Porter was a Yankee sympathizer were somewhat substantiated in testimony she gave the U.S. Court of Claims in 1872 for damages and claims on her vast property. History will probably never really reveal where Madame

51

Porter's allegiance lay, but one certainty remains—General "Dick" Taylor was probably one of the few generals in history who could boast of a victory even though he beat a hasty retreat across the bayou country of Louisiana.[5]

---

[5] Morris Raphael, *The Battle in the Bayou Country*; *Franklin Banner Tribune's 1959 Historical Issue.*

THE HOMESICK SOLDIER

From far back in ancient history to the present time, soldiers on battlefields have often experienced sheer loneliness, and have yearned to be back at home with their loved ones. The following extract, from a letter written February 1, 1864 by a soldier stationed in the Franklin, Louisiana area during the Civil War, tells a touching story.

He wrote: "Let me tell you of a little incident that happened to me while at P.H. (?) this morning. I had been out all day on the skirmish line until about midnight; all was still; I had not heard the singing of a bullet for some time. I was sitting on the ground, with my rifle across my knees, thinking of home and friends far away – wondering what the future had in store for me, and if I should ever see that home again. As I sat thus, a little bird, called the Baltimore Creole, perched himself on a bush so close to me that I might have touched him with my rifle, and commenced singing. The voice of this bird is much like that of our robin, and is about the same size, though his color is different: being a dark red.

"The poor little fellow had been driven away during the day by the shower of bullets that visited that quarter, but had returned at night to visit his home, and seemed now to be returning thanks to God for his safe return. And so, thought I, my case may be like the little bird. After this struggle is over, I too may return to friends and home. I accepted the omen, thanked God for his watchful care over me, and, with renewed courage and hope, pressed on."[6]

---

[6] This excerpt of a Union soldier's letter was taken from *The Boston Herald*, March 23, 1864. The soldier's name is not known.

'THANK GOD, A CONFEDERATE!"

David Hunter Strother was a respected aide and adviser to many federal generals during the War Between the States. A Virginian, he entered the army as a civilian topographer and left the ranks a brigadier general.

In the Spring of '63, Colonel Strother fought alongside Brigadier General Godfrey Weitzel while the 19th Army Corps, under the command of Major General Nathaniel Banks, launched a major attack against Dick Taylor's small army entrenched in the bayou country of Louisiana.

After the heated battles of Bisland and Irish Bend, Taylor's outnumbered forces began an orderly retreat from Franklin toward Vermilionville (Lafayette) and Opelousas, with Weitzel in close pursuit.

Strother had relatives near Jeanerette and had visited them six years earlier. He received permission from the General to see his cousins Mrs. Nancy Weeks and Miss Fanny Hunter who were sisters. He rode ahead of Weitzel's forces, crossed a bridge at Jeanerette, and headed up the bayouside to the home of Alfred Weeks.

There, he discovered Miss Hunter on the porch with a young lady who was her niece – Mary Weeks, a playmate of Strother's daughter during that bygone visit. He learned that Mrs. Weeks had given birth to a child two days before he arrived.

Mary immediately inquired about Captain O.J. Semmes of the gunboat Diana that was captured by the Union forces when Semmes and his crew scuttled the vessel at Franklin. She was engaged to the Captain, and Strother assured her that Semmes was in good health and in good hands. (It was reported that Semmes and Weitzel had been classmates and friends at West Point. Semmes, who was later left loosely guarded, perhaps on purpose, managed to escape.)

Colonel Strother then told in his diary of the tearful reunion when he was invited into the house to see Nancy and her eight children. "I have never seen as strong a picture of concentrated pride, anger, and distress." The women at first refused the U.S. protection, but, under the circumstances, decided to accept it, if there would be no oaths, promises, or conditions. He wrote, "Nancy wept aloud and grasped my hand convulsively. Tears gushed to my eyes, and I covered my face with my hands and sobbed. Those proud, generous, fiery and loving hearts had been of my dearest

56

and earliest friends. I soothed her to quiet and sat down beside her." But Nancy couldn't conceal her loyalty to the southern cause and made an emotional outburst that echoed throughout the household. "Thank God," she exclaimed, "he was born day before yesterday while the Confederate flag still floated here."[7]

---

[7] Cecil B. Eby, Jr. "A Yankee in the Civil War," (*The Diaries of David Hunter Strother*), pages 168, 169, 170, 171, and 172; *1960 Centennial Edition of Morgan City Review*.

AN EMBARRASSING INCIDENT

Union General Nathaniel Banks had an exciting full life, politically and militarily. He served 10 times in the U.S. Congress, was Speaker of the House, Governor of Massachusetts, and a strong organizer of the Republican Party. As a general, he led his forces in many campaigns throughout the nation, including Louisiana battles.

Banks was described as being tall, thin, and heavily mustached. He was also honest, forthright, and usually well liked by his soldiers. However, he was consistently unsuccessful as a technician. On May 11, 1864, an intelligent officer, who had served under General Banks, told the following story about Banks during the construction of the Red River Dam at Alexandria:

"The other day, a man of the 118th New York, who was at work on the dam, suddenly quit his hold on the log he was lifting and commenced damning General Banks instead of the Red River Dam. General Banks was right behind him in his slouch hat, cavalry pants, and flannel blouse, at work shoveling dirt, or something of that kind, and the blackguarding he received was too much for his feelings to bear without notice. So he went over to the New Yorker and took hold of the log himself, saying, "Keep your temper my good fellow; keep cool. Old Corporal Banks has been in many a tighter place than this. He'll get you out all right."

The writer went on to say that the New Yorker was so ashamed and conscience stricken that he related the incident to all he met "as an atonement for his evil speech."[8]

---

[8] From the *Worcester National Aegis and Transcript*, June 18, 1864.

THE CONFEDERATE AMBUSH AT NELSON'S CANAL
NEAR NEW IBERIA, LA.
OCTOBER 4, 1863

MORRIS RAPHAEL

THE BLOODY ENGAGEMENT AT NELSON'S CANAL

During the Spring of 1863, a bloody Civil War raged in the Teche country of south Louisiana. Union General Nathaniel Banks, with a powerful force of three divisions and a fleet of gunboats, overpowered a small army of stubborn Rebels who were "dug-in" on two fronts in West St. Mary Parish.

Confederate Major General Richard Taylor, who was in command of the Rebel forces in western Louisiana, ordered his brave stalwarts to fall back in orderly fashion, but his never-say-die attitude prevailed. He was sure to constantly pester the Yankee invaders with stinging marauding attacks. On occasion, after receiving adequate reinforcements, Taylor was victorious in important conflicts, which included the battles of Bayou Bourbeau, Mansfield, and Pleasant Hill.

There was one engagement near New Iberia, which didn't attract much mention in history books that was unique, dramatic, and cleverly planned. It all happened on October 4, 1863. About 325 Confederates under the command of Colonel William Vincent, 2nd Louisiana Cavalry, who was known for his guerrilla tactics, fell back after skirmishing with a strong force in the Franklin/Jeanerette area. He was determined to make a stand at a partially wooded plantation.

Confederate 1st Sergeant H.H. Connor, an artilleryman of Company A, Spaight's Battalion, was assigned, along with other members of his regiment to bolster Vincent's Cavalry. Connor was also a diarist who wrote an interesting account of the action at Nelson's Canal, described as a "hedge-lined drainage ditch" named after wealthy New Orleans businessman and plantation owner, S.O. Nelson, and located about two miles below New Iberia.

The deep ditch was south of the Bayou Teche and ran about 90 degrees to the bayou. The only passage across Nelson's Canal was a bridge built over a large brick culvert and located about 500 feet from the bayou. Vincent stationed many of his men in the ditch and had them effectively spaced over a distance of about a quarter mile from the bayou to a railroad bed. The rest, who were members of his cavalry, were hidden in a nearby wooded area west of the gully.

In the meantime, his scouts were constantly firing away at the invading Union force of two strong units led by Colonel Harai Robinson's Louisiana Cavalry and Colonel Edmund Davis's 1st Texas Cavalry. The Union troops followed the snipers into Vincent's trap. According to Connor's diary, the invaders were "firing, cussing, yelling, and shouting, on and over the bridge, and when our bugler sounded 'fire,' we opened a crossfire at from 10 to 50 yards, which hushed up the racket very suddenly – and, for some, it hushed it forever."

He continued, "For 10 or 15 minutes, the lane presented a grand scene of confusion, men without horses, horses without riders, dead, wounded men and beasts, men shouting, horses screaming (neighing) with pain, officers giving orders, and the continuous rattle of musketry. All combined made it a grim and fearful scene. To relieve them, a party of cavalry charged down on us from outside the lane, and was not noticed until they had come very close to us. The right of our little line opened on them, driving them back at a gallop, emptying several saddles."

Connor stated that he and several of his party had climbed out on top of the bank to have a better view of the scene near a fence about six feet away. He said, "I saw three men afoot, trying to make their escape. I fired three shots from my pistol, the last shot taking effect, and I was partly on the fence, intending to get over, holding my pistol in one hand by the side of my head. I did not notice one of the men had mounted a horse right opposite me, and seeing me on the fence, fired at me with his sharpshooter, not more than 10 feet away, the ball striking my pistol barrel and glancing aside. At the same time, he put spurs to his horse and probably escaped. By this time, their batteries came up. We were ordered to fall out of the ditch and back to our horses, which we succeeded in doing, but were compelled to continue on in the lane to effect our escape.

"In doing that, we were placed in direct range of their batteries, which were planted by this time on or near the bridge, but we ran the gauntlet of shot and shell tearing up the earth around us. We lost but one man wounded, belonging to the 2nd Louisiana Cavalry, in service of Vincent's scouts. We never knew of the enemy's loss, but it was considerable from the number of dead and wounded seen on the ground. We brought off but one prisoner."

Colonel Vincent, delighted with his successful ambush, led his forces through New Iberia to Vermilionville (Lafayette) and later bivouacked at Camp Pratt. Brigadier General Alfred Mouton, who was assigned the Teche area, sent a communiqué to General Taylor on October 4, stating: "I have the honor to report the enemy at New Iberia. We left the town at sundown. Colonel Vincent ambuscaded them at Nelson's Bridge, and their advance was driven in, leaving the road full of dead and wounded."[9]

---

[9] Morgan City Archives. Dr. Haskell Monroe, Texas A&M papers); Morris Raphael's feature story in *Acadiana Lifestyle's* issue of January, 2009.

A TREASURE OF GUNS

Many years ago, I met a Morgan City, Louisiana postal employee by the name of Tom Torrito who told me an incredible story about a cache of Civil War artifacts, which was found by a friend of his who lived in Berwick, Louisiana. Tom said his friend would paddle a skiff across Berwick Bay and probe around in a tunnel along the Morgan City waterfront where he uncovered Civil War rifles. The rifles were said to be wrapped in oil paper and were in excellent condition.

Tom's friend stored the guns under his home in Berwick and, over a period of time, collected approximately 20 rifles. Unfortunately, the man was killed in the Korean War, and his mother began giving the guns away to friends. Tom had acquired one that he showed to me.

Later, I discovered an old map that showed Fort Star, located in southwest Morgan City, which had a maze of tunnels connecting it with Berwick Bay on the north and Bayou Boeuf to the west. When I saw the map, I wondered what other artifacts might be found in the maze of tunnels.

Incidentally, Fort Star was a large, four-sided fortress, well built and well equipped with a variety of powerful weapons. A portion of this great facility remains today and is easily accessible to the public. Fortunately, the upkeep and preservation of this historic site has been maintained for many years by the Atkinson Memorial Presbyterian Church, which is located nearby.[10]

---

[10] Morris Raphael's interview of Tom Torrito; Morgan City, Louisiana archives.

CAMP PRATT
NEW IBERIA, LA.
CHRISTMAS, 1862

CAMP PRATT WAS AN ACTIVE SITE DURING THE CIVIL WAR

Camp Pratt, which was located on the western bank of Spanish Lake and approximately five miles northwest of New Iberia, was an important Confederate military establishment during the War Between the States. It was the scene of several skirmishes, used for awhile as a prison camp, and was even utilized by Yankees when the Rebels were uprooted from the New Iberia area.

The place was named after Brigadier General John G. Pratt of St. Landry Parish who was in command of the state militia for the parishes of St. Mary, Terrebonne and St. Martin. The camp was then located in St. Martin Parish because Iberia Parish was not created until the year 1868, taking in parts of St. Martin and St. Mary Parishes. According to the late Louisiana historian Powell Casey, reports by the Adjutant General for the State of Louisiana for the periods 1860, 1861, and 1862 indicated that there were as many as 6876 men from eighteen parishes trained in the facility by July, 1862.

After the war broke out, Governor Thomas O. Moore converted the tract into a Civil War training camp for conscripts in Louisiana living south of the Red River and west of the Mississippi. In mid 1862, when General Richard Taylor was assigned to command the Confederate forces in western Louisiana, he immediately developed Camp Pratt into a major camp of instruction. At one time there were as many as 3000 trainees enrolled at the facility.

Union Second Lieutenant George C. Harding of Company F, 21st Indiana Infantry, who was imprisoned for one and one-half months at Camp Pratt, made these comments in his book entitled *The Miscellaneous Writings of George C. Harding*:

"On the morning of the 26th (meaning September 26, 1862), I was started for Camp Pratt on Bayou Teche, in charge of Lieutenant Chamberlain. We landed at New Iberia about an hour before day, a little town with dirty streets, and a strong sheepy smell. After daylight a buggy was procured, and, through a long lane, which had more than one turning, I was conveyed to 'Purgatory,' which in the language of the country, was called 'Camp Pratt,' a camp of conscription and instruction, six miles from New Iberia, and fifty miles from the Bay (meaning Berwick Bay). The camp itself was a collection of plank 'wedge tents' with here and there small editions of the stars and bars flapping their greasy folds in the breeze. I was taken before Colonel Burke. Colonel Burke was the 'big Injun' of Camp Pratt (This was Colonel Ross E. Burke of the 2nd Louisiana Infantry). I was turned over, properly receipted for, and then, after taking a formal leave of Lieutenant Chamberlain, who treated me very kindly, I was escorted to the prisoners' quarters, where one hundred and thirty seven Yankees, taken at Bayou des

71

Allemands, were confined." (Confederate Colonel Edwin Waller, Jr. of the 13th Texas Cavalry captured these men.)

Lieutenant Harding revealed his prejudices as he made the following derogatory remarks about the Cajuns:

"The wants of a Cajun are few, and his habits are simple. With a bit of cornbread, a potato, and a clove of garlic, with an occasional indulgence in stewed crawfish, he gets along quite comfortably, and for luxuries, smokes husk cigarettes and drinks rum – when he can get it. The Cajun has great powers of endurance but not much stomach for fight. Of the herd at Camp Pratt, desertions were quite frequent, sometimes as much as thirty or forty stampeding in a single night. But they would be caught, brought back, made to wear a barrel for a week or two, and were finally broke in.

"Seven of us," Harding remarked, "were stowed in one tent – a dirty, greasy pen, densely populated with vermin. We had three blankets among us and as northers would occasionally blow up, one might imagine our sleep was not 'balmy.' We had about a quarter of an acre of ground for one hundred and forty persons to exercise upon, with a guard of one Cajun, with a double-barreled shot-gun, to every fourteen feet of ground. For food, we had yellow cornmeal, beef, and sugar issued to us, with the alternative of cooking it ourselves or eating it raw. Camp Pratt was short of crockery, and the boys, for plates, used all sorts of contrivances, so that they frequently ate their mush from pieces of gourd calabashes, the shoulder blades of deceased oxen, and other unique vessels.

"While the men had money they would buy milk at twenty-five cents a quart; eggs, fifty cents per dozen; sweet potatoes, four dollars per bushel; a twelve-ounce loaf for fifty cents, etc.; but after they had eaten up their knapsacks, canteens, and in some instances, their shoes, they had to return to mush and beef.

"In justice to the Camp Pratt officers, I must say they gave to us just what they did to their own men. Indeed, I generally found them willing to oblige us, when in their power. One might naturally imagine the days at Camp Pratt were long and irksome. The entire literary resources of our party amounted to an old magazine, a Dutch dictionary, a Catholic prayer book in French, and a well-worn edition of *Robinson Crusoe.*" (Lieutenant Harding was eventually paroled, worked for awhile on *The New Orleans Times* and then returned up North.)

The Confederates suffered a crushing defeat at Camp Pratt in the Fall of 1863. The following excerpt from a report by Yankee Brigadier General Albert L. Lee, who was commanding the Cavalry Division of the Department of the Gulf, describes the action that took place:

"General: I have respectfully to report that on the 20th of November (1863) our front having been on the previous day severely annoyed by the cavalry of the enemy, learning that he occupied in some force Camp Pratt, a point six miles north of your camps, I attempted, under your direction, his surprise and capture. At 2 a.m., the 1st Brigade of this division, Colonel T. J. Lucas, 16th Indiana, commanding the 3rd Brigade, Colonel C. J. Paine, 2nd Louisiana, commanding, and a section of Nim's 2nd Massachusetts Horse Artillery, all under command of Colonel Lucas, moved across the prairie until opposite the flank and in the rear of the enemy's camp,

74

reaching this position, undiscovered, shortly before dawn.

"At 4 a.m., with 300 cavalry and another section of Nim's battery, and supported by the 1st Brigade of Infantry of the 3rd Division, 13th Army Corps, under command of General Cameron, I moved out on the road leading directly from Iberia to Camp Pratt. Just before day, at a point one mile south of Camp Pratt, my advance came on the enemy's pickets, wounded and captured one, and drove the remainder in. I, at once, charged their camp with cavalry, the infantry moving rapidly on their flanks and rear, and, in a quarter of an hour, almost the entire force of the enemy were prisoners. A few escaped through the adjoining woods. We found that their force consisted of 7th Texas Cavalry Colonel Bagby. The colonel was not with the regiment. Our captures amounted to 12 commissioned officers, 100 enlisted men, 100 horses and equipment, and about 100 stand of arms of all kinds. This constituted the effective force of the regiment, which they have claimed was the flower of the cavalry. The Rebels lost 1 killed and 3 wounded; our loss was nothing."

A touch of humor was injected in the Weeks' papers in a description of this place:

"One of the Confederate outposts was called Camp Pratt and was on Lake Tasse (Spanish Lake) and about where the Nickerson Pecan Grove is located. It was the nearest Confederate camp to New Iberia; and for long years after the war, when the older residents wished to discharge the dubious claims of anyone to brilliant military service, they would express a belief that the braggart never went further than Camp Pratt."

It is an historic fact that thousands upon thousands of soldiers utilized Camp Pratt as both Confederate and Union troops surged back and forth across the bayou country of Louisiana. Scores of Yankee regiments from New England and New York used the facilities during their marches, as well as the Rebels from Louisiana and Texas.

This hallowed ground was certainly deserving of the historic marker, which was erected on the site and dedicated with much fanfare on October 4, 1980. Iberia Cultural Resources Association sponsored the auspicious program. It may be well to mention here that New Iberian G.K. Pratt Munson is a direct descendant of General Pratt. It is important to both North and South that the memory of Camp Pratt is preserved to commemorate the many historic activities, which took place there nearly a century and a half ago.[11]

---

[11] Morris Raphael's *Battle in the Bayou Country*; *The Miscellaneous Writings of George C. Harding.*

THE LAST REBEL UNIT TO SURRENDER

(While engaged in Civil War research, I came across an interesting story about Confederate Captain Bailey Peyton Vinson and Union Lieutenant Charles H. Chace, which I felt I should share with you. Most of the material in the following article was extracted from William H. Chenery's regimental history, "The Fourteenth Regiment Rhode Island Heavy Artillery (colored)." Some of the material was taken from Napier Bartlett's *Military Record of Louisiana*. The

Morgan City Archives also provided information.)

After struggling through a bloody and devastating four years of intense warfare, the Confederacy of Southern States reluctantly decided to call it quits. General Robert E. Lee, commander-in-chief of all southern forces, surrendered on April 7, 1865. General Richard Taylor followed on May 9, and a few weeks later on May 26, General Kirby Smith, commander of the Trans-Mississippi Department, also bowed out.

However, there was one Confederate Cavalry Unit in St. Mary Parish, which continued to carry on. It was Captain Bailey Peyton Vinson and his 11th Louisiana Company of Scouts called the "Rough Riders." He and his band of fighters had the reputation of being "dashing and daring" and were recognized as "the best force in the Trans-Mississippi Department."

Although Vinson heard rumors the Confederacy had surrendered, he was in a dilemma – he was not officially notified and hesitated to make a rash decision of laying down his arms. He continued his scouting activities in the Teche region and waited with caution for word from his high command.

Delving into the background of Captain Vinson, we find he was a resident of St. Mary Parish, Louisiana, and entered the service as a lieutenant in Lieutenant Colonel Charles Dreux's Battalion, which was the first military organization from Louisiana to take up arms against the United States government. On the 5th of July, 1861, the gallant Lieutenant Colonel Dreux, with a force of 150 selected men, made a reconnoitering movement toward the Union stronghold near Newport News, Virginia where he was killed in action. Lieutenant Colonel Dreux was said to be the first Confederate officer killed in the war.

Lieutenant Vinson and another soldier, who participated in the engagement, carried Dreux's body off the field and placed it in a wagon. Vinson was then directed to escort his commander's remains all the way to New Orleans where he was buried in the St. Louis Cemetery. Vinson eventually transferred over to the 11th Louisiana Volunteers and returned to St. Mary Parish where he organized his company of Scouts. He was assigned to patrol a large area along the Bayou Teche and Atchafalaya River.

Union General Robert A. Cameron, commander of the Lafourche District Heavy Artillery, with headquarters at Brashear City, was aware that Vinson and his unit had not surrendered and that he needed to have him contained. On June 3rd, 1865, Cameron issued a special assignment to his ordinance officer, Lieutenant Charles H. Chace of Company "A" (colored). He was to take the steamer "Tommy" upstream through the Atchafalaya River and Bayou Teche with adequate troops to find Vinson, inform him of the situation of affairs, and demand his surrender.

Chace immediately followed up on his commander's orders, selected 80 men, carried a flag of truce, left Berwick Bay at 6 a.m., and headed upstream. He passed the wreckage of the Gunboat Cotton above Pattersonville, which was scuttled by the Rebels in an earlier confrontation, and noticed a cloud of dust in the distance believed to be that of Vinson's Scouts. After docking alongside a levee at Franklin, he directed Captain Fry to remain on board and not allow anyone to venture onshore. He then took his servant Billy Valentine with him as they ambled along Main Street in search of the Mayor's office.

Chace wrote the following in his diary: "Not a soul was to be seen, but an occasional movement of the curtains or blinds assured me that our presence was well known to the inhabitants, and that we were being closely observed – for in a moment, without any warning, we were surrounded by about 25 men who seemed to rise up from the ground. They were armed with carbines, revolvers, sabers, and some even having weapons concealed in their boot-legs. To say that I was alarmed feebly expressed my feelings on that occasion, for I was completely in their power had they been disposed to harm me.

"I put on a bold front, however, and, stepping up to the men, I inquired the way to the Mayor's office. The men appeared inclined to treat me civilly and invited me to follow them, and with this escort, I proceeded to the Mayor's office and was introduced to the Honorable A.D. Tucker, Mayor of Franklin. I had a very pleasant conversation with the Mayor, lasting about an hour, and then I inquired of him if he knew where I could find Captain Vinson. I was confident the men in waiting were a portion of his command, and gave Mayor Tucker a copy of my orders.

"He then went outside the building and held a long interview with Lieutenant William R. Collins who had just ridden into town. Lieutenant Collins said if I would return to Pattersonville on my boat, he would guarantee to have Captain Vinson there on my arrival." As soon as Chace got there, he ventured onshore and observed several horses hitched near the levee. He encountered approximately 30 of Vinson's men lounging under trees. He noticed they were well armed with Sharps and Burnside carbines, revolvers, etc. and were in excellent shape "ready for business."

Captain Vinson appeared shortly thereafter in a "cloud of dust" along with Lieutenant Collins, Major Devlin of the "Home Guards," and Captain Louis Wiltz (Wiltz became Governor of Louisiana in 1880).

Vinson gave his frank and thorough explanation of his position, and Chace was touched and did not want to take advantage of an "honorable foe." He decided not to ask for Vinson's surrender until he had an opportunity to communicate with his superiors.

However, Chace offered to accompany Vinson and his officers to Union headquarters to present their case to General Cameron with the promise they'd be returned to Pattersonville unmolested. Vinson accepted the offer, went on board the Tommy, and after arriving in Brashear City, had a satisfactory meeting with Cameron where surrender terms were agreed upon. Vinson and his officers returned to Pattersonville, at which place his company was soon disbanded. Captain Vinson then retired to his plantation, which was located some six miles below Brashear City.

Lieutenant Chace made these remarks about the courageous Rebel captain who evidently became his friend: "It was my privilege to visit him occasionally during the stay of our battalion at Brashear City. I loved to admire his sterling qualities of mind and heart, and could not but observe that he was a true representative of an American soldier, although fighting on the wrong side."

Chace made the following statement, which should have an historic ring throughout our nation: "I am credibly informed that this company of scouts (meaning Vinson's Rough Riders) was the last organization of the Confederacy to surrender." The descendants of Captain Bailey Peyton Vinson and his fighters, and also St. Mary Parish, should be justly proud of the accomplishments of this unique group who maintained their loyalty to the Confederacy right up to the bitter end of the war – and even longer.

CONFEDERATE VICTORY AT AVERY ISLAND

Not long after the War Between the States broke out, the Confederate government found itself in desperate need of salt. This was probably the most valuable commodity, since salt was used extensively in the preservation of meat and was an essential ingredient in the seasoning of foods. It was even used in the manufacture of ammunition.

Prior to the war, most of the salt consumed in the South came from England through the Port of New Orleans. However, this access was eliminated when the city fell, and too, as a result of Union Flag Officer David Farragut's coastal blockade. During this period, a most important salt mine was being developed at Petite Anse Island (now known as Avery Island) located about 10 miles southwest of New Iberia. The small island rises to a height of approximately 170 feet in the midst of a widespread sea swamp. Bayou Petite Anse takes a crooked course from the island to Vermilion Bay.

Judge Daniel D. Avery, a prominent southerner, who was married to Sarah Marsh, owner of most of the island, was developing an elaborate salt evaporating plant, utilizing brine springs, which had been discovered on the island before the turn of the 19th century. Judge Avery was dedicated to Dixie's cause and began developing the plant primarily to supply salt to the Confederate States and Army. In fact, he allowed a number of southern states to establish their own salt works on the island.

However, after a number of operations had gotten underway, it was learned that the amount of brine from the wells was insufficient to accommodate the various operators.

Later, in May of 1862, young John Avery, who was the son of Judge Avery and in charge of production, made a most important discovery. While his slaves were cleaning out and deepening one of the salt springs, they suddenly ran across a tremendous rock salt bed. It was the first rock salt discovery in the continental U.S., and the vein was only 15 to 20 feet below the ground level. Confederate General Richard Taylor, who was in command of the forces in the District of Western Louisiana, learned about the new find through his intelligence and, consequently, Judge Avery placed the mine at Taylor's disposal.

A great many black workmen were then assembled to extract the salt from the mine, and a packing establishment was organized at New Iberia to cure bccf. During the succeeding months, steamers transported large quantities of salt and salt beef to Vicksburg, Port Hudson, and other ports east of the Mississippi River.

By November, the Federal gunboats, after several engagements, succeeded in reaching Berwick Bay, thereby cutting off Rebel shipments. However, General Benjamin Butler, who was in command of the

Department of the Gulf, was anxious to destroy the Avery Island Salt Works. So he ordered the gunboats Diana and Grey Cloud (the Grey Cloud was also known as the "Kinsman"), along with the steamer transport St. Mary's, which was loaded with the 21st Indiana Regiment, to proceed via the Gulf of Mexico, Vermilion Bay, and then up Bayou Petite Anse to destroy the salt works.

The Confederate command received word of the enemy movement and dispatched T. A. Faries' Louisiana Artillery Units to the island. Faries loaded two 3-inch rifles and two 12-pound howitzers aboard the gunboat Hart at Camp Bisland on November 19 and began to proceed to the island by way of the Bayou Teche. Camp Bisland was located about five miles east of Centerville. They reached New Iberia later that day and managed to bivouac nine miles beyond that town near the end of a causeway, which connected the mainland with the island.

The causeway was constructed through a sea marsh and was subject to tidal action. This condition, coupled with the frequent rainfall, caused the roadbed to become unusually soft and boggy and presented a problem for the transfer of field units to the island. The following day, after much trouble and delay, Captain Faries succeeded in making the crossing only after he substituted oxen for the six-horse teams in each carriage.

On Friday, November 21, Union soldiers began landing by means of small boats. As they approached Gaudet's position, "five spherical cases" were fired at the invaders, causing them to disperse and retire rapidly toward their boats, dragging with them a number of their dead and wounded.

The following day, Winchester's units also began firing away at the enemy gunboats, which were visible in the bayou approximately a mile and a half away. After firing thirty-three shots, the battery commander realized that only a few of the shells had managed to reach the target area, so he ordered the section to cease fire and secure a closer position at the bottom of the hill. At this time, Lieutenant Winchester, who was chief of the section, experienced a close call. As the units began to move downhill, a shell from one of the gunboats struck the ground just where the Lieutenant had been posted.

Satisfied that the Union invaders were repulsed, the Confederate command ordered Faries' battery to return to Bisland. On November 24, the units marched back to New Iberia where the sections were placed aboard the steamers Darby and Hart and routed back down the Teche.

The Union flotilla, while withdrawing southwardly through East Cote Blanche Bay, encountered severe difficulties. An extreme low tide, which resulted in a strong norther, caused the vessels to run aground on a shell reef. The small fleet was grounded for over two weeks. In order to obtain flotation, the crew finally had to toss tons of heavy supplies and ammunition overboard. These included coal, chain, cannon balls, Parrot shells, and canister shot.

The Confederate victory at Avery Island, small that it was, was short-lived. Union General Nathaniel Banks, who relieved Butler of his command, continued the invasion of the bayou country with a powerful army of three divisions numbering approximately 18,000 men and 4 gunboats. Taylor's 4000 men fought gallantly at the Battle of Bisland, the

Battle of Irish Bend, and skirmishes along the way.

When the Union forces occupied the New Iberia area in April of 1863, they destroyed the salt works at Avery Island. However, it was apparently a stupid thing to do because they had to rebuild it later in order to utilize it for their own purposes.[12]

---

[12] Morris Raphael's books, *The Battle in the Bayou Country; A Gunboat Named Diana;* and Dave Edmonds' book, *Yankee Autumn in Acadiana.*

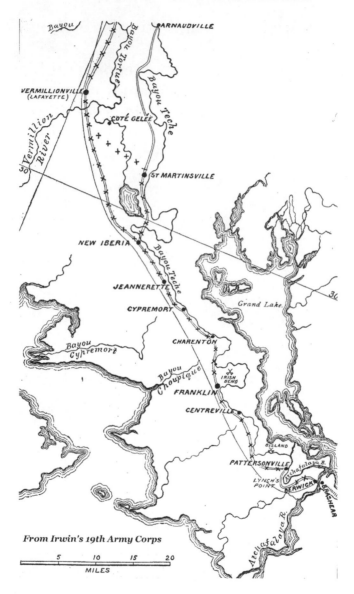

From Irwin's 19th Army Corps

MILES

THE UNFORTUNATE GERMANS

Prior to the Civil War, many Germans migrated to the United States and became citizens. When the war broke out, most of them, feeling an allegiance to the Federal government, enlisted in the Union Army. However, there were some who first joined the Confederates, and then broke away to fight alongside the Yankees. An interesting, but sorrowful story was published in a regimental history of the 8th Vermont Volunteers. It was reported that seven Germans who had enlisted in the U.S. regiment at New Orleans were among prisoners captured by the Rebels at Bayou Des Allemands in 1862.

The seven soldiers were recognized by some members of the Confederate Guard, arrested as deserters, and then executed. The report stated "the men had protested their utter innocence of the crime laid to their charge, and pleaded that the act of enlistment was an exercise of their rightful privilege as citizens of the United States." It was further stated that the captors would not listen or show them any mercy, or allow the Germans to communicate with their friends, or prepare for their defense. A court martial was then held "which went through a farce of hearing testimony and returned a quick verdict of guilty."

The report continued with the information that the men were marched to a point under some trees beside a railroad track where a long trench had been dug. Here, they were arranged in such a manner that when shot, they would fall into the trench. Seventy Confederate soldiers were summoned with their muskets to do the job, but several were unwilling and hired substitutes. However, unknown to any of the executioners, a blank cartridge was placed in one of the rifles, and when the Germans were shot at, it left a consoling doubt as to just who did it. The story stated that the warm bodies were hastily thrust into the open grave and just enough dirt was thrown upon them to hide them from "the face of the accusing sun." It is mentioned that an aged, heartbroken father shoveled the dirt away from the smoldering remains of his only son, a handsome lad, and said, with tears rolling down his cheeks, "It is hard to let him go, for he is all that I have."[13]

---

[13] George Carpenter's *History of the 8th Vermont;* Morris Raphael's *The Battle in the Bayou Country.*

A PLEASANT EXPLOSION

General Richard Taylor lived an ultra-active military life, which was replete with victories, defeats, and frustrations. His background could possibly have been the envy of any southern officer. Taylor was the son of former President Zachary Taylor, the brother-in-law of Confederate President Jeff Davis, a member of the Louisiana Legislature, and the owner of a sugar plantation in St. Charles parish.

This Louisianian fought his heart out for the Confederacy. He was a hero in the Virginia campaign, and in the Spring of 1863, although he was overpowered by a strong Union Army and Navy in the bayou country battles, he held and evaded his enemy in an amazing strategic move. He later won a smashing victory at Mansfield.

At the war's end, Lieutenant General Richard Taylor, who then held command of the Department of Alabama, Mississippi, and East Louisiana, met with Union General E.R.S. Canby a few miles north of Mobile to establish a truce. He stated that he arrived on a hand-car, powered by two blacks and was met by General Canby "with much urbanity..." On April 30, 1865, they retired to a room where they agreed on a truce.

At this time, we can imagine Taylor's dire disappointment and sorrow, for he was one who went to extremes, always trying desperately to lead his forces to victory – and, now, the war was over, and the Confederate Army had surrendered. Throughout the war, he continuously experienced the roar of cannons, shells exploding, and the crack of rifles. In his immortal book, *Destruction and Reconstruction*, he wrote the following about a luncheon with Canby and several other Union officers:

"A bountiful luncheon was spread, of which we partook, with joyous poppings of champagne corks for accompaniment, the first agreeable explosive sounds I had heard for years. The air of 'Hail Columbia,' which the band in attendance struck up, was instantly changed by Canby's order to that of 'Dixie,' but I insisted on the first, and expressed a hope that Columbia would again be a happy land, a sentiment honored by many libations."[14]

---

[14] Richard Taylor's *Destruction and Reconstruction*; Morris Raphael's *The Battle in the Bayou Country*.

The Battle of Vermilion Bridge
Vermilionville, Louisiana
April 17, 1863

THE BATTLE OF VERMILION BRIDGE

As Confederate General Richard Taylor and his small army made a successful exodus from the hot field of action at Irish Bend and Bisland in St. Mary Parish, Louisiana (June 13 and 14, 1863), they headed in a northwestwardly direction seeking a safe haven.

However, as they retreated, they destroyed whatever they thought would be of use to their enemy. A few miles below New Iberia, the powerful gunboat Hart, which was in an unfinished state for battle, was scuttled crossways of the Bayou Teche as an additional obstruction to the powerful Federal fleet.

The fleeing Confederates also set fire to several transports laden with stores, and with the Yankees right on their tails, they crossed the Vermilion River and set fire to the bridge as quickly as possible. However, in their haste, Taylor's men lost three of a train of 30 wagons. But the Rebels not only stopped the Federal forces from crossing, they also prevented them for repairing the bridge. This was April 17, 1863. There was only one thing left for the stymied Yanks to do and that was to drive Taylor out of his position of strategic advantage. This would then enable the invaders to throw a pontoon bridge across the bayou.

Captain Henry Closson, U.S.A. Chief of Artillery, advanced to the skirmish line of the 6th and began hammering away at his enemy—a distance of about 1500 yards. Later four guns from Nims' battery supported him. The battle of Vermilion Bridge lasted for about four hours, with apparently no great loss in dead or wounded on either side. Taylor, satisfied that most of his troops and train were a safe distance ahead, picked up his wounded and moved out of range of heavy Yankee fire.

This had been a weary day for the Federal forces who had marched 20 or 30 miles over a hot, dusty trail, trying desperately to catch up with the Rebels, and now they welcomed the chance to rest on the high banks overlooking the Vermilion. The following day, while awaiting the construction of the new bridge, nearly half the Yankee force decided to take advantage of the opportunity by stripping and bathing in the bayou.

Suddenly, without an instant's warning, a troop of Taylor's cavalry dashed down the opposite bank and opened fire on the naked men. This is how one observer described the scene:

"Such a spectacle never before was seen. The long roll was sounding and naked men, in every direction, were making a dash for their guns, trying to dress as they ran. Some, with their trousers on hind side before; didn't know whether they were advancing or retreating, and some ran the wrong way; others, with simply a shirt and cap, were trying to adjust their belts. Officers were swearing and mounted aides were dashing about, trying to make order out of confusion."

Taylor resumed his retreat at noon, April 17th, while the Feds were still obsessed with the problem of crossing the bayou. The Confederate forces, which were now well rested, passed through Opelousas and Washington on the 18th and 19th. Colonel Green's rear guard cavalry maintained its effective role of retarding and frustrating the Yankee operations. On the following day, Taylor found himself with all his trains behind the Bayous Cocodrie and Boeuf.

On the 20th, Mouton was ordered with all the cavalry, except Waller's battalion, westward to Niblett's Bluff, on the Sabine River. Then Taylor, along with Colonel Waller and the column of worn infantrymen, continued their steady retreat toward Alexandria, halting the main force at Lecompte. Again, Taylor used his most effective defensive tactic – he burned the bridges at the Cocodrie and Boeuf.

On the morning of April 19th, Union General Nathaniel Banks, satisfied that the pontoon bridge across the Vermilion had been constructed, took off again after Taylor. The village of Vermilionville, now known as Lafayette, was described as being a town of some 300 inhabitants, with two churches and a convent as its principal buildings. One thing soon apparent to the Yankees was that the name Mouton represented important leaders of the community. On entering the village, the soldiers passed the elegant residence of ex-Governor Alexander Mouton who was the president of the convention that caused the secession of the state. Nearby, stood the home of the brave General Alfred Mouton, who combined his strategic talents with those of Taylor in executing the amazing withdrawal from the Franklin area. From almost every house, the people hung towels, pillow cases, and handkerchiefs as flags of truce.[15]

---

[15] Henry Goodell's *25th Connecticut Volunteers;* Richard Irwin's *19th Army Corps*; Morris Raphael's *The Battle in the Bayou Country.*

A PROUD SOUTHERN LADY
STRIKES BACK

In the late 1970's, right after I wrote my book, *The Battle in the Bayou Country*, I received a delightful letter from a man in Florida by the name of John Parkerson, who happened to be 92 years old at the time. He told me a fascinating story about his great-grandmother who lived in St. Mary parish – how she waded into a band of wild Yankees who invaded her plantation. Later, while reading through a New Hampshire regimental history, I ran across an item that corresponded with that very same incident. The following is a combination of both items, which I felt made an interesting story.

While the Yankees were marching through East St. Mary parish, an exciting incident occurred. Elated with victory, resulting from the Teche campaign in the Spring of 1863, the soldiers became undisciplined, fell out of column, and began foraging. Some entered a plantation and began shooting and chasing chickens and turkeys. Lieutenant Colonel O.W. Lull, who was the Union Provost Marshal, had the marauders driven back to the road, except for a long-legged Indiana boy, who disregarded the loud command of the colonel and continued to chase and beat a huge turkey.

The incensed mistress of the place came out with a buggy whip and waded into the culprit. The colonel raised his revolver and sent a bullet through the soldier's regulation hat, saying, "Stand still, my man, I'll shoot lower next time." The soldier abandoned his booty, fled through a fence, and disappeared in one of the columns. The southern matron was profuse in her thanks to the colonel, and, as a token of her gratitude, begged him to accept the turkey, which was almost dead. Colonel Lull was delighted to receive the gift, which he transferred to his orderly's saddle-bow, and the column marched on to its destination.[16]

---

[16] Parkerson's letter; Morris Raphael's *A Gunboat Named Diana*; John Stanyon's *History of the 8th Regiment*, New Hampshire vols.

YANKEES TAKE OVER
NEWSPAPER

In October of 1863, after the Union army chased the Confederates out of the bayou country, several troops occupied New Iberia. One of the soldiers of the 130th Illinois Regiment, who happened to be a printer by trade, was walking through town when he noticed a printing shop that was "abandoned and desolate." Since the door was locked, he climbed through a window and began to tinker with the equipment.

The proprietor of the building arrived soon thereafter and politely presented the Yankee with keys to the building. Other printers from the Federal army came forward and they published their first newspaper entitled "Unconditional Surrender, U. S. Grant," on October 24, 1863. It was printed on wallpaper as was commonly done during that period because of a paper shortage. The newspaper, which was printed before this, was called, "The Confederate States," and, of course, it was a Rebel newspaper.

The Yankee newspaper appeared to be newsy. One item of local interest was that "Brigadier General Pratt and 14 other Rebels passed through this place a few days ago as prisoners of war en route to New Orleans. They were captured near Vermilionville by the

1st Texan (Union) Cavalry." The Union army utilized much of New Iberia's facilities and products as the war raged on.[17]

---

[17] Union newspaper entitled "Unconditional Surrender U.S. Grant," October 24, 1863.

YANKEE GUNBOATS CLEAR BAYOU TECHE NEAR JEANERETTE, LOUISIANA (APRIL, 1863)

THE RICHARDSONS VALIANT VENTURE

There are two well-known antebellum homes just west of Jeanerette that were owned by brothers during the Civil War. Francis Dubose Richardson owned Bayside, north of Bayou Teche, while the home across the bayou belonged to John Westley Richardson. They were successful sugarcane planters.

In 1863, when the Richardsons found out that Union gunboats were headed upstream, they felt an obligation to do something for the Confederacy. They planned to convert the floating bridge, which connected their properties into a fiery obstacle. They piled stacks of brush and timbers on the deck and saturated it with pitch. When the Union fleet was approaching, the bridge was set ablaze and allowed to float downstream. The brothers had high hopes that their efforts would block the Union advance.

But, unfortunately for the Richardsons, it was an easy task for the invaders, who shoved the fiery bridge to the side with long poles and continued their upstream invasion.[18]

---

[18] Richardson Family History.

CHICKERING'S SIX MILE TRAIN

In May of 1863, after the Yankees had conquered the Teche region of south Louisiana, some Union forces, with the help of black labor, began confiscating products, which included cotton and sugar, and shipping it by boats to New Orleans. One report revealed that over 400 bales of cotton were in a shipment. However, the draining of bayou country resources continued in another big way by land. Union Colonel Thomas E. Chickering of the 41st Massachusetts Regiment, who had been appointed governor of Opelousas, was directed to organize, collect, and lead a wagon train shipment to New Orleans.

Nearly everything of value was confiscated and placed in wagons for the long haul. These consisted of ammunition, beds, bedding, furniture, cooking utensils, cows, geese, cotton, tobacco, sugar, molasses, artillery, horses, mules, beef, and approximately 6000 contrabands. The belongings of these slaves were piled high on the wagons. Throngs of blacks joined the swelling column as each plantation furnished its quota to the black multitude. Harris Beecher's *History of the 114th New York Regiment* wrote this:

"In the history of the war, it is probable that another such sight was never witnessed. There can be no doubt that this was the greatest multitude of contrabands ever collected. Every few minutes the boys would burst into shouts of merriment as some new scene, especially ludicrous or ridiculous, presented itself. Here came a mammoth plantation cart filled with rough furniture, and screaming children, nearly nude, drawn by a pair of oxen. Then came a young man leading a cow, upon whose horns and back were attached a rattling museum of frying pans, pails, gridirons, old clothes, and hoes. Next appeared a creaking wagon, in which was an old grey-haired couple, demurely sitting on a broken stove. Then came trudging along a bevy of barefooted women with infants, papoose-like on their backs. Presently, a very ancient and ragged looking mule had two or three women and children astride its back.

"Again would appear more plantation carts covered with awnings of blankets, cowhides or boards. Then the attention would be attracted to an old man limping along on a cane and carrying a half-naked child astride his neck. Or the eye would fall upon a young wench

114

walking stiff and erect with an enormous bundle poised upon her head. Occasionally, an old vehicle would break down on the road and scatter in the mud the most wonderful furniture, furnishings, clothing, and traps generally that the mind can conceive of. Now and then, some quaint establishment would have a runaway, tearing through the black ranks, upsetting everything in its mad career."

There were many more exciting and comical occurrences during Chickering's six-mile journey to his destination. No doubt, there were sad situations as well. His wagon train was labeled "The Freedom Train," and was, perhaps, the longest of its kind ever in the U.S.A.[19]

---

[19] Morris Raphael's *The Battle in the Bayou Country*; Harris Beecher's *History of the 114th New York*.

A SACRED FLAG

At the beginning of the Civil War in 1861, excitement broke out all across the bayou country of Louisiana. A beautiful young lady, Louise McKerrall of Franklin, delivered a stirring speech on the courthouse grounds to a newly formed artillery unit. She presented the group with an attractive flag, which bore the words, "From the Ladies of Franklin to the St. Mary Cannoneers," and said dramatically, "Return with it, or may its folds forever shield you."

Unfortunately, the flag was captured by the Union's 13th Connecticut during the bloody battle of Irish Bend, near Franklin, on April 14, 1863. It fell into the hands of Major C. Kinncy who brought it back with him to Connecticut. As time went by, Major Kinney's wife became more and more sympathetic and felt the flag should be returned. "It was with pride," she said, "and it waved over the heads and hearts of fearless men."

A resolution was introduced in the House of Representatives at Hartford and passed on February 19, 1885, directing that the flag be returned to the veterans of the St. Mary Cannoneers. When the news reached the Veteran Association of Franklin, the whole village and surrounding country were thrilled

with excitement. An elaborate reception was
held and was especially heartwarming since
the charming Mrs. Louise Chambers (the
former Miss McKerrall) was present during
this historic event. Mrs. Kinney became the
recipient of many exquisite gifts and much
grateful appreciation from the southerners.

The flag was then sent to the Confederate
Museum in New Orleans for safekeeping.
However, in 1959, Rev. Jerry Tompkins, a
Presbyterian minister in Franklin, found the
flag in the possession of the Louisiana
Historical Association in New Orleans. He led
a civic group to the city and made an appeal
for its return to Franklin. The appeal was
granted, and the flag was deposited in the St.
Mary Landmarks Museum in Franklin, but
since the precious banner was in a serious
state of deteriorating, officers of the
organization became very concerned.
However, two dedicated members, Robert
Judice, Jr. and his wife Carolyn, brought the
flag to a New Orleans fabric preservationist
where it was given a thorough anti-
deteriorating and preservative treatment. It
was also framed.

The flag is safe and is now exhibited in the St. Mary Landmarks Museum. This precious remnant has survived a horrible battle, the adverse elements of time, the shuffling to and fro across our country, and stands today as a reminder of the brave men who fought and died for a cause that they thought was right.[20]

---

[20] Morris Raphael's book, *The Battle in the Bayou Country*; Louisiana History and Landmarks Archives.

COURAGEOUS REBEL

There were no submarines involved in the bayou country Civil War campaign, and there was very little mention that torpedoes or mines were utilized. However, two well-known Franklin, Louisiana men, Confederate Lieutenant Donaldson Caffery and Daniel Dennet, who was editor of the *Planter's Banner* newspaper, devised a torpedo with the intention of blowing up a Union gunboat that was docked at the Brashear City (Morgan City) wharf.

Their homemade torpedo consisted mostly of a heavy stone jug filled with black powder, tightly corked, and attached to a long pole. At the appointed time for their daring adventure, Lieutenant Caffery, half-naked, plunged into Berwick Bay, swam across to the other side, pushing his torpedo-attached pole ahead of him until he reached the boat. Fortunately, he was unnoticed.

He then shoved the pole under the vessel and pulled on a rope that was attached to a trigger. Unfortunately, instead of exploding, the torpedo slipped off the pole and sank to the bottom of the Atchafalaya River.

Since there were armed sentinels walking their posts from stem to stern aboard the vessel, Caffery had to be very careful. He grabbed two floating logs, hid his head between them, and gradually made it back across the Bay where Dennet was waiting with a horse that had no saddle. Caffery rode horseback for eight miles to the place where his clothing had been deposited. Since it was a chilly night, he caught a bad cold and suffered many years thereafter with rheumatism.

Only a few friends knew of Caffery's courageous adventure until after the war when he became a U.S. Senator. His exciting story was then partially published.[21]

---

[21] *St. Mary Franklin Banner Tribune's 1959 Historical Edition*: "The John Caffery Papers."

BATTLEFIELD DRUNKS

From ancient history up to the present time, it is an historic fact that military people on battle fronts have often overindulged in consuming alcohol as a nerve soother and relaxant. Although commanders issued strict orders for soldiers to refrain from drinking the demoniac substances, they, too, were frequently guilty. The American Civil War had its share of alcoholics. The following stories reveal some of the unfortunate cases. Here are extracts from a letter written by a Yankee soldier who was stationed at Gentilly, Louisiana in February, 1863:

"The bane and destroyer of an army is whiskey. Citizens at home can have little appreciation of the enormous amount consumed by the soldiers. A little stimulant under pressure is absolutely necessary. But of this class, I have nothing to say. They are answerable only to themselves. How this evil may be remedied is not for your correspondent to write. This same whiskey causes nearly all the trouble, which officers meet with..."

An article in the *Boston Journal*, dated April 28, 1863, tells a very interesting story. Major General Benjamin F. Butler, who was commandant of the Federal Department of the

Gulf during the early phases of the Teche Campaign, and a man who was labeled "Spoons Butler" and "Beast Butler" by Louisianians, was asked the following question by the Union Committee on the Conduct of the War. "Are intoxicating liquors used in the Army?"

"They are," he said, "to a woeful extent. We used to send a picket guard up a mile and a half from Fortress Monroe. The men would leave perfectly sober; yet, every night we would have trouble with them on account of their being drunk. Where they got their liquor from, we could not tell. Night after night, we instituted a vigorous examination, but it was always the same. The men were examined over and over again, their canteens inspected, and yet we could find no liquor about them.

"At last, it was observed that they seemed to hold guns up very straight, and upon an examination being made it was found that every gun-barrel was filled with whiskey – and it was not only the soldiers who do this. I ordered a search of the Adams Express Company and examined the packages sent to the soldiers by their friends, and in one day, I have taken one hundred and fifty different packages from the trunks, boxes, and packages sent to the soldiers by their sympathizing friends at home."

Confederates were no less guilty. The following incidents occurred during the Spring of 1863 when the Federal forces were approaching New Iberia. While the Rebels were in the process of evacuating via the St. Martin and Vermilion routes, there was some display of stubbornness and wild patriotism within the ranks. Lieutenant Colonel I. D. Blair, who was under the influence of Louisiana rum, made it known to those around him that he was going to fight the whole Union army single-handed.

Although he was told that over 5,000 Yankees were approaching the city, he still maintained he could whip them all. His regimental friends, however, became quite concerned about the welfare of the colonel and came up with a unique plan. Someone in the ranks challenged Blair to a horse race from New Iberia to St. Martinville. He accepted the offer and started out of town on a full run. The scheme saved the colonel the anguish of being captured by his enemy.

Another Confederate soldier who had drunk too many toasts to the ladies that morning and who also wanted to take on the entire Union army by himself was Ed B. Talbot of Iberville parish. Talbot bravely exposed himself to the Federals who were drawn up in line of battle of approximately one hundred yards in width and who were gradually approaching the town. In fact, Talbot rode in front of the Union ranks, calling them names and daring them to fight. The Federal regiments held their fire for fear of hitting the women and children who were exposed in the background.

After much difficulty, his buddies succeeded in convincing him to fall back, telling him that he was ordered to take charge of an ambush in the rear. It was reported that Talbot lived to be one of the best lawyers and judges in the state, and, at the same time, "setting an example of sobriety and general rectitude."

But the heavy drinking was not only done by soldiers and lower grade officers – even generals were guilty. One example was that of Confederate General Henry H. Sibley, a Louisianian who had a long career of leading

126

forces in battles across the nation. He was labeled a "notorious alcoholic" by at least one historian.

Perhaps Sibley's drinking brought on problems he experienced in the Teche Campaign when he was in charge of the forces at Fort Bisland during the Spring of 1863. His commander, General Richard Taylor, tried to have him court martialed for disobedience and unofficial-like conduct. However, Sibley was acquitted of the charges.

History tells us of many, many cases, too numerous to mention, of overindulgence on the battlefronts.[22]

---

[22] Morris Raphael's *Battle in the Bayou Country*; Mark Boatner III's *Civil War Dictionary;* T. Michael Parrish's *Richard Taylor, Soldier Prince of Dixie*; "The Weeks Papers," New Iberia Parish Library.

THE LAST CASUALTY OF THE BATTLE OF BISLAND

Confederate General Alfred Mouton, a native of Vermilionville, Louisiana (Lafayette), and the son of Governor Alexander Mouton, fought courageously under the command of General Richard Taylor. In late November, 1862, he hurriedly had a fort built in a strategic location along the banks of Bayou Teche between Centerville and Pattersonville (Patterson), which was called Bisland in honor of Dr. Thomas Bisland who donated a large tract of land for the Confederate cause.

The fort was built in an effort to stop the powerful penetration of the Union Army and

Navy that had conquered the Berwick Bay area and were gearing up for an all-out invasion of the bayou country of Louisiana. On April 12, 1863, a terrific artillery battle erupted, which involved the incessant firing of cannon balls and Parrot shells. During the night, the overpowered Confederates withdrew their forces to a safer location.

After the war, several sugarcane farmers built houses in the Bisland vicinity, and modern-day artifact hunters, as well as others, have found numerous unexploded ammunitions used by both sides. According to the late David Stiel, Franklin historian and insurance entrepreneur, an awful tragedy occurred at the Bisland site. He said a young lady by the name of Eula Mae Blanco, who lived there, lost a leg. It happened that on a cold day when she was warming herself near the fireplace, a twenty-pound Parrot shell, which was used as a grill support, exploded.

David said, "The young lady was the last casualty of the Battle of Bisland, and used crutches the rest of her life. She died in 1989." David warned people who discover these shells to be very careful because the black powder may still be active and could explode when heat is applied.[23]

---

[23] David Stiel interview; Morris Raphael's *The Battle in the Bayou Country,* and *A Gunboat Named Diana.*

THE SOLDIER AND THE SQUIRREL

The following story was extracted from a Union diary. An infantryman by the name of Philip Souder Holmes of Stockton, Maine, who was a private in the 26th Maine Volunteer Regiment, tells of an unusual and lasting friendship that existed between him and a wild animal.

In April of 1863, Holmes left Brashear City aboard the transport "Laurel Hill," which was part of General Cuvier Grover's fleet during the invasion of Irish Bend. He wrote: "We landed at Indian Bend under a heavy fire from field pieces stationed behind an old sugar house. Some of us were wounded and some had to be looked out for. As for me, I had a fox squirrel, which I caught at the Battle of Irish Bend." He wrote that a shell from the Rebel "Gunboat Diana" struck a tree and knocked down a nest of young squirrels. He caught one and placed it in his haversack. The squirrel not only became tame, he became a regimental pet.

Private Holmes was wounded at Irish Bend, but the squirrel, which was tucked snugly in the breast of his coat, refused to leave him, even while he was interred at the hospital. During the Battle of Port Hudson, while Holmes was lying in the trenches, the squirrel would leave for a good while, but as soon as the guns started firing, the tiny animal would return on the run and dive into Holmes' haversack. Before long, the squirrel became so tame that he would go the entire length of the regimental line, jumping from shoulder to shoulder of the men, but he would always return and creep into Holmes' haversack where it would sleep.

When the war came to an end, Holmes was delighted that he was able to bring his beloved friend all the way back to his faraway home and farm in Maine. Here, the little pet was given the freedom to roam across the fields and into the woods. However, each day when it came time to sleep, the squirrel would return to his favorite nesting place, which was the same old haversack that Holmes wore in the Louisiana battles. The haversack hung on the corner of the chimney place, which was a safe haven the animal used for the rest of his life.

It is believed that there are probably many descendants of the little squirrel that was

CIVIL WAR VIGNETTES OF ACADIANA

rescued and adopted during the Battle of Irish Bend roaming the woods of Maine today.[24]

---

[24] Philip Holmes's diary – 26th Maine Volunteer Infantry.

AMERICANA – A CONFEDERATE HAVEN

My wife, Helen, and I met in Santos, Brazil in 1957. She was Director of Courses for the United States Information Agency, and I was project engineer of a Carbon Black plant. We had made a lot of friends, and in 1986 we decided to return for a visit. It was a wonderful experience – we had a ball.

But ever since I wrote my first book, *The Battle in the Bayou Country*, I had been anxious to make a trip to a settlement called Americana, which was a few hundred miles northwest of São Paulo. Many ex-Confederates who refused to live under Yankee rule chose a life elsewhere. Americana is a colony, which has sustained the elements of time and maintained its heritage and southern lifestyle.

We made our trip by bus to the home of Mrs. Judith McKnight Jones, author and grand dame of the colony. After a delightful and informative visit there, we toured the area and were taken by taxi to the expatriates' cemetery, which included a church and a recreation hall.

Our hosts explained how the cemetery came into being. In the early days, the Americans were not allowed to be buried in the regular Brazilian cemeteries because the space was reserved only for Catholics. The early settlers were predominantly Protestants and, according to newspaperman Tom Murphy, they were looked upon as heathens. So, the Americanos were forced to provide their own site – a place that has grown to large proportions. At one time Brazilians were not allowed to be buried there, but over the years, the rule was relaxed due to intermarriages.

The array of ancient tombstones attracted me to no end, and I could hardly wait to check 'em out. I left Helen 'way behind as I weaved my way in and around, backwards and forwards, looking desperately for Louisianians. Tracking down this lost colony of Confederates did something strange to me. Goosebumps began to break out all over my body, and I could swear that I heard strains of "Dixie" playing. The huge headstones were probably carved from the nearby mountainsides, and the inscriptions were in English. Some, affected by the elements of time, were hardly readable. I passed up familiar names like Porter, Fox, Provost, Buford, Young, Burns, Tilly, Grady, Davis, Shaw, Moore, Vincent, Doherty, Kramer, Stiel,

CIVIL WAR VIGNETTES OF ACADIANA

Carter, Rader, Myers, Kennedy, and a hundred or so more. I could have spent an entire day just eyeballing the stones, but I knew my group was tiring and ready to return. But, just as I was about to leave, I discovered, much to my joy, two tombstones in a row, indicating graves of people born in St. Mary Parish, Louisiana. They were: Mrs. Pamela Coulter, wife of Dr. D. Coulter, born June 22, 1848, who died July 19, 1878; and Martin Felix DeMaret, born September 2, 1818, who died July 21, 1893; and a third tombstone read, "Sarah Lee DeMaret, daughter of Colonel M.F. and Mrs. Pamela Z. DeMaret, was born in Grimes County, Texas, August 5th, 1861 and departed this life February 8th, 1874 in Ste. Barbara, Brasil."

I surmised offhand that Sara Lee and Pamela Coulter were daughters of Martin Felix DeMaret. Helen and I returned to São Paulo that night with the glowing feeling that we had experienced a wonderful adventure. We had made friends with real southerners so far away from home who were actually Brazilians, and I had interesting work cut out for me to delve into the genealogy of three important graves that I discovered near Americana, Brazil.[25]

---

[25] Morris Raphael's *My Brazilian Years.*

THE BRAVEST OF THE BRAVE

Strange things do happen. A Yankee was proclaimed and respected as one of the bravest Confederates during the bayou country Civil War campaign. He was Emelius Woods Fuller, a native of Lawrence County, Ohio, who settled in the St. Martinville area, became a State Representative, and established a sawmill and shipbuilding industry at Chicot Pass in the Atchafalaya Basin.

When the Civil War broke out, he led a company of volunteers called the "St. Martin Rangers," which was referred to as "Fuller's Company Bull Battery." He then converted a large river steamboat, "The Cotton" into a powerful gunboat, which was known by the Union forces as "The Terror of the Teche."

Although Fuller had fought courageously in several land skirmishes, his big heroic encounters began in November, 1862, when a fleet of four Yankee gunboats invaded Berwick Bay. Fuller, as Captain of the Hart, fought bows on with the powerful Union armada. He eventually backed his vessel up Bayou Teche to a point near Cornay's Bridge. After several discouraging encounters, Lieutenant Commander Thomas Buchanan, leader of the Union fleet, decided to withdraw his gunboats to Brashear City (now Morgan City) and wait for infantry support on the bayou banks. Fuller then became Captain of the Cotton. The Cotton's resistance gave Confederate General Alfred Mouton time to build fortifications in the Bisland area.

On January 13, 1863, Buchanan, with the aid of land units, moved his armada toward Cornay's Bridge where the Cotton was poised for battle. The gunboats blasted away at each other. Buchanan, who exposed himself carelessly, was killed by a rifle shot, which came from a rifle pit. The fierce battle raged, and casualties mounted on both sides. The Union's heavy guns, which were said to total approximately 27, proved disastrous to the Cotton, and the brave Captain Fuller, who fought courageously, holding back the four powerful gunboats, was shot in both arms. He worked the wheel of the vessel with his feet as he backed out of action.

Lieutenant E.T. King, who replaced Fuller, was ordered to scuttle the Cotton crosswise in the bayou as a major obstruction to the Union gunboats' upstream attack. He burned the vessel and sank it as ordered. Fuller, who was hospitalized in Franklin, recovered from his

142

wounds, got back into action, and converted vessels into gunboats. On April 14, 1863, while the bloody battle of Irish Bend raged, he was in command of the "Queen of the West" when he was confronted by three Union gunboats.

A hot battle got underway during which a percussion shell hit the Queen, exploded, cut a steam pipe, and set fire to the vessel, which sank. Although about 40 members of the crew drowned, many were rescued, including Captain Fuller. He was then imprisoned and conveyed to Fortress Monroe, Virginia. On June 10, 1863, Rebel prisoners aboard the steamer "Maple Leaf," overpowered the guard and escaped. But Fuller, who was one of the prisoners on board, ill and weak, chose not to escape for fear of jeopardizing the safety of the escapees.

Fuller died while a prisoner on Johnson Island, Lake Erie, on July 25, 1863. He was admired and respected by the Confederate hierarchy for his outstanding gallantry. Major General Richard Taylor, who was in command of the District of Western Louisiana, stated that "Captain Fuller was a western steamboat man, and one of the bravest of the bold." He also recommended that Fuller be bestowed "some kind of favor for his single-handed gallantry in defeating four gunboats."[26]

---

[26] Morris Raphael's *A Gunboat Named Diana*, and *The Battle in the Bayou Country*; Richard Taylor's *Destruction and Reconstruction*; Richard Irwin's *History of the 19th Army Corps*.

STUPID ATTACK – GREAT RESULTS

After the Union forces conquered the bayou country of Louisiana, they engaged in skirmishes, foraging, confiscations, and even the wanton destruction of property. During December 1863, the Yankees planned an attack on a large plantation and farmhouse that was located several miles west of New Iberia on a high plateau overlooking a beautiful lake. The place was known as Miller's Island (today, it is known as Jefferson Island).

The Union command had heard that there were approximately 80 Confederate pickets located at the home site and also felt that the high elevated land would be a strategic area for military observation posts. The Yankee invaders were composed of forces from Harai Robinson's 1st Louisiana Cavalry and Benjamin Thurber's mounted 75th New York Dragoons. Their attack was well planned.

Before dawn, the Yankee troops moved cautiously and quietly to the island and set up their positions within 50 yards of the big house. At the appointed time, at sunrise, Captain Thurber gave the signal for the men to attack from all directions. The soldiers shouted as loud as they could, bugles blasted, sabers and guns were thrust, and without firing a shot, the soldiers broke open the doors, shattered windows, and rushed into the house.

The wild invaders were utterly surprised and ashamed. There were no Rebel soldiers – only a small family of four who were frightened out of their wits. They were Faustin Dupuy, his wife Mary, and their teen-age sons, Adam and Alcee. When Dupuy regained his composure, he told the intruders he was a Union man and hadn't seen any Rebels for weeks. He then invited the officers to join him at breakfast.

The Union troops liked what they saw in and around the mansion. There were oranges galore and orchards of figs, peaches, quince, lemons, and palms. They also discovered a fine herd of cattle, lots of chickens, and the barns overflowed with corn and oats.

The Yankees collected a generous sample of each, and Mr. Dupuy gave away several thousand cigars. When the troops returned to New Iberia with their booty, other soldiers envied what they saw and made plans to do more foraging at Dupuy's place.[27]

---

[27] David Edmonds' *Yankee Autumn in Acadiana*; U.S. Court of Claims: "Faustin Dupuy vs. the United States;" James Hall's *Cayuga in the Field*.

YANKEES BEWARE

The Yokely Bridge, which was located just west of Franklin on what was known as "The Harding Cut-off Road," figured prominently in the Confederate forces simultaneously withdrawing from two battle fronts – the one at Irish Bend, and the other at Bisland. This happened on April 13, 1863. The Rebels fought gallantly against great odds. Their forces numbered less than 4,000, while the Yankees, with heavy land and naval power, were estimated to have approximately 18,000 men.

During the bloody fighting at Irish Bend, a brave Union Colonel, Edward L. Molineux of the 159th New York Volunteers, was shot in the mouth and carried off the field. He survived, became a general, and commanded valiantly the remainder of the war. About 137 years later, Morris Raphael, the author of this book, and his wife Helen, offered to take the colonel's great-grandson, Will Molineux and his wife, Mary, on a tour of the bayou country battlefields. (The Raphaels had struck up a friendship with Will several years earlier. He is a prominent Williamsburg, Virginia columnist and historian. His wife, Mary, is a librarian at the William and Mary University).

The Molineuxs accepted the invitation, and after they arrived, were shown the approximate spot in a sugarcane field where the colonel fell in battle. Although it began to rain, Raphael was determined to complete the last lap of his tour, which was at the Yokely Bridge site. It was still raining when they reached the place, and Raphael decided to park on the side of the road.

Unfortunately, he parked on a freshly dug spot where a storm sewer had been laid, and the front end of the car sank to the axle. He said he felt like crying. Adding to their misery, the rain came down in torrents, and they were helplessly trapped for an hour or so – which felt like ages. Finally, a city work truck came to their rescue and pulled the car out of the quagmire.

Will, who has a good sense of humor, remarked, "Morris, it appears as if the Confederates have cast a spell on this place. They're getting back at us Yankees for what happened a long, long time ago."

The frustrated and disappointed foursome returned to the Raphaels' home where the Molineuxs were served a Cajun seafood gumbo, which the Raphaels had concocted.

They all relaxed and began talking about their hectic experience. There was even a suggestion made that a sign should be erected: "Yankees Stay Away from Yokely." They laughed about it all.

THE YANKEE JUGGERNAUT

A very revealing report of Civil War activities in the Teche campaign was written by a Union scribe for the *New Orleans Era* newspaper. It was published on April 28, 1863. The writer was stationed in the "Field" above New Iberia. A portion of the article is as follows:

"On Sunday morning, the 12th instant, the whole division (meaning Union General Cuvier Grover's) embarked on board the gunboats Clifton, Calhoun, Estrella, and Arizona, and the transports St. Mary, Laurel Hill, Quineboug, Southern Merchant, and Segur. Proceeding up the bay, through Grand Lake Pass and Grand Lake, by a cross bayou, they reached Irish Bend, on the Teche bend like that of an ox-yoke, about three miles west of Franklin.

"The 1st Louisiana Regiment was the first to land. It hardly stepped ashore when an attack was made upon it by the Rebels with two pieces of artillery and 200 infantry. Some were killed on both sides during the firing, which immediately followed. The enemy were (sic) compelled to fall back. Upon reaching the Teche, several rifle shots were fired by the Rebels. They attempted to prevent the approach of our troops. This attempt likewise failed before the sharp firing of our men, and the Rebels were driven still further back. Our men crossed the Teche and bivouacked for the night.

"The next morning at an early hour, they started toward Franklin. While marching along the levee road, upon reaching a point two miles from Franklin, on which is called Irish Bend, they again met the enemy. There was a cross road meeting the main, and in this their artillery was planted, commanding all the country about there. As the troops came up, up to their right was a thick forest of large trees, behind which the enemy was concealed, having a wooden fence between them and their opposers.

"Preparations were made at once for a desperate attack. As one of their number, now a prisoner, remarked, 'Know that we got to fight hard, or be taken prisoners.' The 25th Connecticut Regiment was the first to engage the enemy. It occupied the center of the line of battle. The 26th Maine Regiment was on the right and the 13th Connecticut Regiment on the left, and was supported by the 12th Maine regiment. It was deployed as skirmishers on the left of the road, and thus marched until abreast of the woods. And then, while under a sharp fire from the enemy, the line gradually swung around till it faced the woods, letting the enemy get to their rear.

"Then an attempt was made to capture our artillery without success, although the regiment gradually fell back, until it received support from the 91st New York. The 25th Connecticut was ordered into action on the left of the line and in advance. They met the enemy awaiting their approach in a piece of woods, where their artillery was supported by a strong force of infantry and cavalry.

"When a charge was ordered to force the Rebels from their position and to take their artillery, the 3rd had to charge through a ploughed field and over two fences. Notwithstanding these obstacles, this regiment succeeded in capturing two caissons, six horses, two swords, and a splendid flag from the enemy. The flag was of fine silk, six feet in length, bordered with rich silver tinsel, and bore the inscription, 'The Ladies of Franklin to the St. Mary Cannoneers.'

"Soon after the charge of the 13th, the enemy fell back defeated. The force opposed to us was not large, but had advantage of position and of making a surprise attack. The total force of the Rebels, both here and at the batteries below did not exceed 10,000 men. Our loss was considerable, and that of the enemy must have corresponded with ours."

(Author's note: This battle was known as "The Battle of Irish Bend." General Taylor's forces at Bisland and Irish Bend hardly exceeded 4,000 men.)[28]

---

[28] From a field report by a Union scribe, published in *The New Orleans Era* newspaper on April 28, 1863. Morris Raphael Archives.

THE TALE OF THE GUNBOAT HART

After the Confederates were uprooted from the Franklin area as the result of two battles there – "The Battle of Bisland," and "The Battle of Irish Bend," General Dick Taylor became very concerned about the Yankee advance up the Bayou Teche. He managed to keep his forces a safe distance ahead of his foes and, at the same time, to destroy ammunition dumps, burning stockpiles of cotton, scuttling boats, and doing away with anything that would be of use to the enemy.

The gunboat Hart, which had been in service earlier, was being revamped and reconditioned in New Iberia and was to take on the new name of "The Stevens." It was described as one of the best and fastest gunboats in the Rebel navy, carrying one 32-pound rifled cannon forward, a similar cannon aft, and two small smooth-base, 24-pound brass pieces under her casement. Her machinery and bulkheads were protected by three-inch railroad iron, the heaviest kind in use. She had two splendid engines aboard, which were of 20-inch cylinder, seven-foot stroke. There were four double-flue boilers on the boat. But, in spite of the fact that the Stevens had been worked on for a three-month period, Lieutenant Joshua Humphreys, who was in command of the gunboat, reported to Taylor that the vessel was in an unfinished condition and unfit for action.

Taylor, fearing that he would have a problem keeping the boat out of reach of the Yankees, ordered the Stevens to be sunk five miles below the city as an impediment to the ascending Federal gunboats. This was April 15, 1863. But Taylor was angered and disappointed that Lieutenant Humphreys had the boat scuttled only two miles below New Iberia. It was actually sunk in front of Eugene Olivier's mansion, which was located about three miles below the city, but it proved to be an effective plan because the upward thrust of Yankee gunboats was stopped until the wreckage was cleared by demolition units on October 9th, almost six months after the scuttling.[29]

---

[29] *Official Records, Vol. XV.* Morris Raphael's *The Battle in the Bayou Country*. Richard Taylor's *Destruction and Reconstruction*.

SINNERS AT CAMP

During the Spring of 1863, while Union soldiers occupied different towns in the bayou country of Louisiana, they were apt to write to relatives and friends back home, telling them of their experiences and about how different things were in Louisiana than they were up North. The following are excerpts from a letter written by Samuel Garrigan, a member of the 1st Indiana Artillery, which was stationed in New Iberia.

"Dear Friend, I embrace the present opportunity to address you – I am writing in my shirtsleeves, and I am very comfortable. I reckon it is quite different in Indiana, for I suppose it's quite cold there. You will see by reference to the map of Louisiana, we are about 160 miles west of New Orleans, and we are in the midst of fine country – it is called the Teche Country. We are camped on Bayou Teche.

"I find the camp abounding in every kind of vice and corruption. I find it more difficult to live a Christian life here than at home – being deprived of family prayer. But I do not forget to lift my heart to God in prayer each night after going to bed, and I wish you to remember me constantly in your prayers, that

I may live as a consistent Christian though I am in the Army.

"It is thought by some that a man in the Army cannot be a Christian, but I beg leave to differ with them. I have had the opportunity of being at Church twice since I have been down here, and I expect to embrace every opportunity that offers itself.

Affectionately, Samuel Garrigan."[30]

---

[30] Letter by Samuel Garrigan of the 1st Indiana Artillery. Raphael Archives.

The Gunboat Battle at Cornay's Bridge Fought Near Pattersonville, LA. Jan. 14, 1863

THE CORNAY FACTOR

The Cornay family name is ancient. Records reveal there were mighty Cornay warrior knights who participated in the Crusades. There is even a small village in France between Paris and the Belgian border named Cornay. Descendants in the United States also proved to be prominent, patriotic, and progressive. In 1812, a 12-year old descendant by the name of Numa Cornay, settled with his parents in St. Mary Parish in the vicinity of Calumet Plantation. Their home and farm were located on the west bank of Bayou Teche, about five miles west of Patterson. He eventually became one of the wealthiest sugar planters in the parish.

Numa was the father of eleven children, the youngest being Florian Octave Cornay, born in 1832, and a graduate of a military college in 1853 with the rank of Captain. After taking a course at West Point for approximately six months, he returned home at the age of 23 and was named Surveyor of St. Mary Parish. He purchased a home just east of Franklin, got married, and when the Civil War broke out in 1861, he organized the St. Mary Cannoneers with mostly sugarcane farmers from his area – a unit which proved to be very heroic and highly regarded by the Confederate command.

During the 1862 invasion of the New Orleans area by powerful Union gunboats, a bloody cannonading battle occurred on the Mississippi River at Forts Jackson and St. Phillip. Mutiny occurred among several Confederate units, but Cornay's Cannoneers stood fast and held their own until they finally surrendered honorably. It was reported there were no Louisianians involved in the mutiny.

Florian and his men were praised and honored royally. Lieutenant Colonel Ed Higgins, who was in charge of the forts, reported the following: "I wish to place on record here the noble conduct of Captain F.O. Cornay's Company, the St. Mary Cannoneers, which alone stood true as steel when every other company in Fort Jackson basely dishonored its country."

Captain Cornay continued to serve with honor under Confederate General Alfred Mouton, as well as other commanders in many battles and skirmishes in the bayou country campaigns. Unfortunately, in 1864, he was shot and killed during a fierce engagement with Yankee gunboats at the junction of the Cane and Red Rivers. He was buried in nearby Cloutierville. He was revered by the highest officers in the Confederate command for his consistent acts of bravery.

Members of the Cornay families continued to thrive for many years in varied careers such as medical, political, publishing, postmastering, soldiering, agriculture, historical, industrial, property-owning, and were highly regarded in their communities. In a recent study, it was noted that there are hardly any signs of Cornays living in St. Mary Parish. Most have moved away, and names have been changed through marriages.

The old Cornay homestead at Calumet was destroyed by fire by the wild Yankees who invaded the area in 1863, and, it appears, the bridge that linked the east and west bank across Bayou Teche is no longer there. Cornay's Bridge was constantly recorded by Yankee and Confederate scribes, for it was the site of important bloody gunboat battles. And now, after almost two centuries, all that remains of this historic bridge are a few pilings, which are reminiscent of that proud and courageous family who gave their all for posterity's sake.[31]

---

[31] *The Cornay Family Papers;* Morris Raphael's *The Battle in the Bayou Country.*

YANKEES CONVERT EPISCOPAL CHURCH INTO HOSPITAL
NEW IBERIA, LOUISIANA
OCTOBER, 1863

A FAMOUS ANTEBELLUM CHURCH SURVIVES

The Episcopal Church of the Epiphany, which adorns Main Street in New Iberia, is one of the oldest Gothic Revival churches in the State of Louisiana. It not only survived the adverse elements of time but also bears interesting Civil War history.

It was back in 1848 when a small group of three adults and three children became the first townspeople to become Episcopalians. Bishop Leonidas Polk, who later became known as the famous "Fighting Bishop of Louisiana," baptized them. He attained the rank of Confederate Major General during the Civil War and was killed during the Battle of Pine Mountain, Georgia in 1864.

The Rev. Mike Adams, a former rector of the church, stated, "You can't talk about Epiphany without taking in account its historic nature." After the Union Army conquered the bayou country of Louisiana in 1863, the soldiers, led by General Nathaniel Banks, camped inside the sacred building and desecrated it to a great extent. The wild Yankees took out the pews, burned some of them, mutilated the windows, and covered the walls with unsightly charcoal sketches and inscriptions.

Many pews were placed together on the outside lawn to form troughs for the feeding of the soldiers' horses. During the Union occupation, the church was also used as a guardhouse for the prisoners and a makeshift hospital for Union troops.

The Church of the Epiphany stands today, as a reminder of that tragic era when Americans were fighting Americans, and it is also a monument to the various congregations for their staunch dedication to the

preservation and upkeep of their precious
house of worship.[32]

---

[32] Feature story by Diane M. Moore and Francis Manning
in the October, 1994 issue of *Acadiana Lifestyle Magazine*;
The Daily Iberian feature, October 6, 1998; and Morris
Raphael Archives.

THE PRIEST GOT SPANKED

There were many strange stories that erupted as the result of the Yankee conquest and occupation of the bayou country of Louisiana. During the turbulent years of 1863-1864, Fr. Ange-Marie Jan, who was then minister of St. Martin of Tours Catholic Church in St. Martinville, was victimized on several occasions by the wild invaders. They stole much of the priest's livestock and were unusually cruel in their behavior.

Fr. Jan, an elderly 63-year old, was revered by his community for his charitable works, especially for the sacrifices he made during the Yellow Fever epidemic of 1855 when he remained at his post attending to the afflicted masses while others fled. But the Civil War rustling of his six well-bred horses and another by one of his slaves was a heartbreaking experience for this fine person.

While the Union soldiers were in the act of stealing the priest's pets, he made a frantic plea for them to stop. He presented them with papers signed by Union General C.C. Washburn, which states that the Padre was a native of France and was not affiliated with the war. They laughed at the minister and dragged down the French flags, which were unfurled and attached to the balconies.

When an officer began putting the reins on one of Fr. Jan's favorite horses, the priest became infuriated. He, along with a beadle (church helper), lunged at the Yankee and wrestled for awhile, but they were both subdued. The offended officer, red-faced and breathing heavily, then proceeded to administer a severe beating to Fr. Jan's backside with the flat of his saber. One report stated he was also kicked.

Adding injury to insult, when Fr. Jan's female slave and her daughter were caught hitching up a buggy, the priest asked, "What are you doing? I don't have any calls to go out." She answered, "The soldiers said this belonged to me." When Fr. Jan tried to unharness the horses, the soldiers held him back. Other horses were stolen by neighboring slaves. Fr. Jan had a tough time of it all. Even with all the horse-stealing going on, four soldiers followed the priest, demanding that they be wined and dined. Confederates also did some foraging on the church's property.

During May of 1883, Fr. Jan sued the United States Government, through the French and American Claims, for his losses from April, 1863 – November, 1864. He claimed compensations for the Yankees taking his thoroughbred horses, hogs, and 170 barrels of corn. After much debate and testimony during the French and American Claims Commission trial, Fr. Jan, on October 8, 1883, was awarded $850 with interest at five percent from January 1, 1865.

Fr. Jan died on August 15, 1887 and was buried beneath the floor of the sacristy of St. Martin of Tours Catholic Church. His congregation who loved him dearly erected a statue of the saintly priest in front of the church.[33]

---

[33] French and American Claims Commission Records; David Edmonds' book, *Yankee Autumn in Acadiana*; Governor Henry Watkins's book, *The Conduct of Federal Troops in Acadiana*; St. Martinville historian James Akers.

BAYOUSIDE SNIPING

Frank L. Richardson, who resided at the Bayside mansion just west of Jeanerette, Louisiana, wrote a memoir of his Civil War experiences with his squad as they fired away at Yankees along the Bayou Teche. He stated it was March, 1864 when Union General Nathaniel Banks, with a large army, came marching from New Orleans. Richardson and his group were stationed on the west side of the bayou, while the Confederate rear guard covered the opposite bank.

He wrote: "After I rode past the Weeks Plantation, our nearest neighbor, the ladies were out at the roadside waving goodbye as I passed. On reaching my own front gate, I waved goodbye to the family, while the enemy's cavalry was galloping after us on the opposite side of the bayou. At the next place above, the ladies of the family came out to the road to speak to me, when the Minnie balls from the opposite side fell upon them. They seemed to think the shots were not for them."

Richardson stated that two miles further up the bayou, their neighbors, the Thompsons and Dungans, were on the gallery waving at them when one of his enemy's cavalrymen shot at him. He said he returned the shot, hurried up a short distance, and fired more shots. After the war ended, one of the ladies told him that he had wounded a Yankee at that place. After reaching New Iberia, he said he crossed the bayou and found the Confederate troops had gone up toward St. Martinville, except for about a dozen scouts under the command of scout Ned Smith.

Richardson then rode below New Iberia and saw the Federal advance guard drawn up in line of battle at least one hundred yards in width, "and quietly waiting for us to get out of the way. They were near enough, but did not fire at us for fear of hitting the women and children."

Frank Richardson's memoir appeared in two lengthy supplements in the *Louisiana Historical Quarterly* under the title "War As I Saw It." He wrote that it took him over 20 years of peace to muster up sufficient courage to "go over these old wounds that were healed."[34]

---

[34] Frank Richardson's "War As I Saw It," *Louisiana Historical Quarterly*; Morris Raphael Archives.

THE BELL OF THE GUNBOAT DIANA – A MYSTERY

All of a sudden, historians from across our nation have become vitally interested in a bell said to have been rescued from the Confederate Gunboat Diana. Perhaps I should start from the beginning:

Back in the early 1940's, while I was a young member of the U.S. Corps of Engineers stationed in Franklin, Louisiana, I met a fine gentleman by the name of Pres Gates who was very knowledgeable about area history. We would occasionally meet at Rousseau's Coffee Shop on Main Street, where I enjoyed listening to his interesting stories. He told me about the Gunboat Diana, which was sunk in Bayou Teche along the Franklin waterfront during the Civil War. He said that the St. Mary's Episcopal Church needed a bell, so his grandfather, Alfred Gates, who was one of the church's founders, had the bell taken from the Diana and erected in the church's belfry.

Deacons of the church and old-timers of the community told me the same story. I became so interested that I began researching the history of the Gunboat Diana and learned the vessel was scuttled on April 14, 1863. I then wrote feature stories about this subject for magazines and newspapers and eventually published two books about the Teche campaign. A while back, Clarkson Brown, Jr., a Franklin insurance man, a Civil War enthusiast, and an active member of the church, submitted photographs of the bell. It was plainly marked, "Buckeye Bell Foundry, cast by G.W. Coffin and Co., Cincinnati, Ohio, 1864." This threw everything out of balance since the Diana was scuttled in 1863.

Dr. Horace Beach, Ph.D., of Clayton, California, became intensely interested in the Diana and the bell, especially since his great-great grandfather, Private Moise Deslattes, was a member of the crew at the time the vessel was sunk. He contacted various people and agencies in the Franklin area and gathered all the information he could. These included Clarkson Brown, Historian; Margie Luke, City Planning Director; Neil Minor, Director Roland Stansbury of the Young-Sanders Center; and others. Dr. Beach even made a special trip to our area and conducted a comprehensive study of the Diana's history in every way possible. We enjoyed a splendid visit with Dr. Beach and his wife DeAnna at our home in New Iberia. In view of all our contacts by letters and telephone calls over the past few years, Dr. Beach and I have become great friends.

He has written two fine, hardbound books relating to the Diana. His recent work is entitled *The Last Moments of the Gunboat Diana And Her-Almost Final Resting Place.* In this book he states: "This description alone (meaning that of the bell), barring any type of unusual post-dating, rules out the possibility that it came from the Diana." He cites Patrick Hreachmack's remarks that the bell did not look like the kind that a boat would have used.

Mr. Hreachmack, incidentally, is a maritime expert and maker of superb miniature ships and boats, and lives in Lakewood, New Jersey. He is also very interested in the Diana and has created a miniature of the vessel. He, Horace, and I have been in contact with each other. Dr. Beach and Mr. Hereachmack both remarked that the "4" in 1864 appears to have been altered.

I do respect the findings of these two gentlemen, but I am inclined to believe in the information that was originally obtained: Pres Gates' story; and a letter published in the Episcopal Church newspaper, *Churchwork*, in

177

1989, by his sister, Helen Gates Rossner. The letter stated that the bell was taken from the Diana and she "grew up loving it." Ms. Rossner also said that after her father died, her sister, Ms. Amoret Gates Womack, had the bell reworked because it "had clapped for so many years in the same spot that it had to be turned and electrified."

In addition to the above, it is quite possible the numeral "4" was so worn down that the metalist who reworked the bell in later years accidentally made a "4" out of a "1." And, as previously stated, why would the Rebels rig up a vessel with a new bell after they had been defeated? Furthermore, I've always found church records to be quite reliable.

It appears that Horace, Patrick, and I have taken roles as history detectives, trying to solve a mystery about something that happened almost a century and a half ago. Of course, we're all speculating, and unless something positive shows up, we'll never know what actually happened. But there is something I'm certain of – there's a big, beautiful, ancient bell hanging in the belfry of

St. Mary's Episcopal Church in historic
Franklin that rings out loud and clear.[35]

---

[35] Morris Raphael's story about "The Bell of the Gunboat
Diana – A Mystery," *The Daily Iberian* newspaper,
October, 2010.

A PIN "BROKE THE ICE"

Union Colonel Edward L. Molineux of the 159th New York Volunteers led his regiment valiantly in several bayou country engagements in 1863. During the battle of Irish Bend near Franklin, he was shot in the mouth, carried off the field, and hospitalized in New Orleans. After his wound healed, he was anxious to get back into the thick of the struggle where he received several important assignments.

In 1864, he became Commissioner for the Exchange of Prisoners in Vermilion parish and was stationed in the home of a lady whom he described in a letter as "Madam Cade, a proud southern woman of the old Creole regime." He also stated that the lady had been very wealthy, owned a plantation, and, because of the war, she had only "the barest necessities of life. She was a good hater, scorning the Yankees, and spoke to me only when it was her duty to do so.

"She apologized in a queenly way for the little she had to offer me to eat, mentioning that the coffee was compounded from gunpowder and molasses, a very curious drink, and hoped I would like the cornbread. Her Negroes waited upon me, and her little daughter, Lelia, aged ten, was not at all afraid of Yankees – and seemed to like me."

Colonel Molineux stated that none of the things brought from Europe by the Confederate blockade runners ever reached the people west of the Mississippi, and "so this little girl was dressed in an old patched blue frock. She had no stockings or shoes, but wore sandals of cottonwood, laced to her knees with old twine and fastened together with thorns – which, of course, scratched her legs.

"One day," he wrote, "I happened to find a pin in my clothing. I took out one of the thorns in her sandals and replaced it with this pin. This so delighted the child that I sent to our lines for a whole paper of pins and dangled them before her eyes. She was fairly dazzled by so much riches. She rushed to her mother with them, then ran outdoors, and springing on her pony, rode ten miles to give half of them to her aunt.

"This episode brought the mother to me with the first softened expression I had yet seen on her face. Holding out her hand to me, she said with exquisite courtesy, 'Sir, I thank you for these pins. You are indeed a gentleman.'"

(Colonel Molineux was later promoted to General, and at the end of the war was highly honored by members of his regiment, Union officers and friends.)[36]

---

[36] Letter taken from the Will Molineux Archives, Williamsburg, Virginia.

THE SAFE HIDING PLACE

Charles Etienne Gayarre, noted Louisiana historian, legislator, and judge, was a native New Orleanian of distinguished Spanish and French ancestry. During the Civil War occupation of the New Orleans area, he and his wife became afraid the Yankee foragers would sack their elegant home and take off with their precious possessions, so they made plans to do what their neighbors were doing – to hide their treasures in a safe place underground.

Judge Gayarre packed in a secure tin box all he considered most precious to him – his wife's jewelry and diamonds and his treasured heirlooms; his shoe buckles and sword hilt studded with brilliants that belonged to his father; his grandmother's miniature in a frame surrounded with diamonds; de Bore's snuff box; in short, all the priceless, innumerable trinkets that had been kept in his family for generations.

He then set out at night, accompanied by his wife, and selected a good spot under a tree that he could easily identify afterward. By the light of a lantern, they dug a hole in the ground where they buried their priceless treasure. But, as Judge Gayarre stated: their "most accomplished valet and rascal" spied on them and watched the burial of the treasure. On the following morning, the Gayarres were shocked to learn their supposedly loyal servant, William, had dug up the treasure and disappeared with it, along with a carriage and horses. It was learned that William had sold the loot to members of a Union camp and lived on the proceeds for years.

Another judge was more successful in hiding his valuables. He secretly buried a quantity of family silver and gold in his yard and built a chicken pen over it. When the war was over, he unearthed all of it. It was evident that many families buried their treasures during that tragic period.[37]

---

[37] Dr. Herman Seebold's *Old Louisiana Plantation Homes and Family Trees;* Alcee Fortier's *Louisiana.*

Union General Nathaniel Banks Celebrates Occupation of the Shadows-on-the-Teche New Iberia, Louisiana – April, 1863

WARFARE'S TRAGIC RESULTS

Union Captain John G. Mudge of the 53rd Regiment of Massachusetts Volunteers published a book in 1893 entitled *Stories of Our Soldiers* that revealed horrible accounts of the bayou country campaign. Some excerpts that he wrote are as follows:

"It was mid-April, 1863, and the Union forces were in high spirits following their victories at Bisland and Irish Bend near Franklin." He stated that when his regiment reached the outskirts of New Iberia at nightfall, there were over a half-dozen Rebels lying dead on the side of the road. This, he said, was the result of an advance unit a few hours earlier.

He wrote, "The spot of the skirmish was a beautiful plantation, the home of one of those old French families who, in the past, had added luster and renown to the history of the state. But in consideration of the well-known hostility of the owners to the Union, and that the Rebels had fired from this house upon our advance, the boys were allowed to go through it, sack, pillage, and destroy every article within its walls.

"One who has never seen a house sacked by the boys can have no idea how faithfully they do their work. They were at it while we were marching by to our camping ground for the night, which was about three miles distant." (It may be well to mention here that in all probability the house mentioned was not The Shadows-on-the-Teche. The Weeks, Conrads, and the Moores, were Anglo-Saxons, and the mansion was not pillaged.)

On the following day, Mudge returned to the house where all the ravaging occurred and went ahead of his regiment to examine the destruction. He said it was a quaint old house filled with rich, old furniture and costly china imported from France. "But what a wreck! Every article was broken, destroyed, or removed by some careful hand of a Union soldier."

Mudge looked around for something worth carrying away as mementos and couldn't find anything except a few small articles. He wrote, "As I passed into the back court I saw madam, the lady of the house. She was at the foot of a tree with only one attendant. All the men had fled. Her long white hair hung loosely on her shoulders – a perfect picture of despair, hatred, and rage with the ruin, which surrounded her. A feeble attempt on my part to say a word met with no response."

Captain Mudge bought a horse for nine shillings from one of the stragglers, and after a hard ride for a couple of hours, he caught up with his regiment where he claimed he was cheered by his men. But the situation wasn't that rosy at Port Hudson where Mudge's regiment was ordered to charge the Rebel works. He stated, "Company F rose up manfully, and with heroic bravery, charged up the parapet until nearly every man who reached the brow of the hill was either killed or wounded.

"Colonel Kimball, who stood in the bottom of the ravine, seeing us fall back, ordered me again to charge. I replied that I had not a man standing to charge. He was satisfied we had done all that could be required of us. But oh! What a sad sight and a painful time I had in dragging out the wounded of my brave company. Never shall I think of that sad scene and be happy. Out of 34 men who followed me into battle, 22 were killed, wounded and missing."

Captain Mudge was mustered out of service September 2, 1863, and died in Boston March 22, 1891.[38]

---

[38] Captain John G. Mudge's *Stories of Our Soldiers.*

AN UNUSUAL BATTLEFIELD

When The Yankees launched their attack upon Fort Bisland in April, 1863, they ran into conditions to which they were not accustomed. A scribe from the 114th New York Volunteers recorded that his regiment camped just west of Pattersonville (Patterson). Thirteen days before his regiment's encampment at Pattersonville, Rebels had captured the Gunboat Diana in a bloody engagement.

He stated that the decaying mules and horses, which were killed by gunfire from the Gunboat Diana, gave off a terrible stench. He wrote, "Many of the men bundled up in blankets around the campfire, would periodically curse the miserable odor and make shouting demands upon the commissary to 'remove those rations of meat.'"

Union General Nathaniel Banks, along with several of his top officers, decided to join his forces and lead them into battle. Unaccustomed to marching through sugar cane fields, the soldiers found the drive rather tough. Because of the war, the cane was left unharvested, and as the Yankees penetrated the fields, maneuvering through the tangled stalks, row by row, leaping over ditches, they found themselves exhausted and disorganized until they finally emerged into the clearings.

By then, the Gunboat Diana, now flying a Rebel flag, was hurling Parrot shells in their direction with deadly accuracy. The Yankees were puzzled when the Diana would suddenly appear around the bend, open fire, and then disappear. However, they later learned that it was all a clever Rebel trick. The gunboat was tied to a long rope, and when this was loosened, the boat would drift out into the open. After her guns were fired, the Diana would then be pulled back out of sight of the invaders, but the constant shelling by the Yankees put the gunboat out of commission in bloody engagements. Since Taylor's troops were getting overpowered, he ordered a general withdrawal of the Fort Bisland area during the night of April 13, 1863, and ultimately managed to get his little army safely out of reach of the Union juggernaut. On the following day, the Diana was scuttled just above Franklin as an obstruction in Bayou Teche.[39]

---

[39] Morris Raphael's *The Battle in the Bayou Country* and *A Gunboat Named Diana*; Flinn's *Campaigning with Banks*; Irwin's *19th Army Corps*; Beecher's *History of the 114th New York Volunteers.*

CHRISTMAS SPIRIT AND A
MAJESTIC BEAR

It was during the Civil War, Christmas Eve, 1863, in the bayou country of Louisiana, when Colonel Edward L. Molineux of the 159th New York Volunteers, stated in a letter that he and his regiment took time off from the rigors of war to celebrate the blessed event. The Colonel was an exceptionally courageous and well-revered Union officer – he had such a friendly manner that even many bayou dwellers liked him.

He described his tent as being decorated with "a little sprig of holly and evergreen," and that he had spent "the last evening" with a Roman Catholic curate of New Iberia. He stated the priest's name was Father Joseph and that "the old gentleman became so much excited over his cups that he danced, hooted, and sang to an extent far beyond his dignity."

The Colonel wrote, "It is a bright, cold day, and we welcomed it by a beautiful reveille by a full band. The men in camp are comfortable and have a ration of whiskey given each, in honor of the day, and as little work as possible. The box has arrived. To each of the poor darkies hanging around headquarters, I gave a pair of socks."

Molineux mentioned in another letter that the Lieutenant Governor of the State of Louisiana (Henry M. Hymans) presented him with a fine bear cub that was playful and good-natured. He wrote, "I have decided he prefers the benefits of a liberal southern education for his growing mind, so I have given him to the regiment. The drum corps has him in charge, and he is a great favorite and attracts undivided attention. On grand occasions and parades, he marches majestically, at the head of the regiment, with the whole drum corps beating the march behind him.

"At those times," he continued, "he has a fancy for the naked shin bones of young darkies and snaps so lively at them that our road is effectually cleared of their presence. He is now so large and fat that he is troublesome to manage, but the boys would not part with him under any circumstances."[40]

---

[40] Thanks to my good friend William Molineux, the great-grandson of the Colonel, for copies of Colonel Molineux's letters. Will is a prominent Williamsburg historian and columnist. Colonel Molineux was later promoted to General.

PLEASURABLE MOMENTS ALONG THE WAR TRAIL

Confederate Sergeant H.N. Connor of Colonel J.B. Liken's battalion wrote an interesting diary. He told of a heartwarming event as battle weary members were entering Opelousas. He stated, "We met a company of about 50 little boys, all armed with Confederate flags, headed by a priest. Near St. Martinville, our company was presented with a flag by some ladies who were strangers to us. As we passed through Franklin, ladies came on the sidewalk with lemonade and cool water for us."

Connor also wrote, "While at Vermilionville (Lafayette), our principal amusement was hunting bee gums and blackberries. The ladies of this place deserve great credit for their kindness to our sick. The Methodist Church was turned into a hospital, also a number of private houses, and the ladies attended them all that was in their power. Mrs. Mouton (the former governor's wife) acquitted herself as a southern lady should toward a sick soldier. She had received the blessing of many a poor "gray-breeched Rebel, even if some of them did steal her spoons."

******

In 1863, a Union invasion-bound fleet of gunboats plowed through Grand Lake in the Atchafalaya Basin at a slow pace toward the Irish Bend area. The soldiers on board one of the vessels became bored and had a desperate yearning for coffee. One of the men, Joe Pray, had a brainstorm and came to the rescue – he had a novel way in which to make hot coffee. Nearby was the escape-pipe of the steamer, which rose ten to twelve feet above the deck from which hot steam was constantly emerging.

Pray poured a handful of coffee grounds into his canteen and partially filled it with water. He then managed to toss the canteen into the current of steam, holding the container by a long white string. In a few minutes, he withdrew the canteen, which was steaming with the hot refreshing drink. Immediately, coffee makers sprang up all over the ship as Pray's system was copied. From that day forward, Joe Pray was looked upon as a hero and a genius.

******

J.P. Moore of the 52nd Massachusetts disclosed a humorous incident about the Federal cavalcade passing through St. Martinville in May of 1863. "Two ladies," he wrote, "were sitting very haughtily on their upper gallery observing the passersby. Suddenly, their colored "mammy," weighing about 250 pounds, rushed out of the lower part of the house and set out to join the parade. The haughtiness of the fine ladies on the gallery changed. They flashed down the inner stairs, rushed to the very edge of the street, got each a fat arm of their household reliance, and

sought to drag her back to the house. The soldiers cheered both sides – but the two ladies prevailed."
******

In March of 1863, after the Federal Gunboat Diana was captured as the result of a three-hour bloody battle with Rebel land units near Patterson, Louisiana, acting Captain Harry Weston surrendered to Major H.H. Boone of Waller's Texas battalion. One of the Texas Rangers, who couldn't wait to be transported over to the Diana, swam over to the vessel and let out an Indian war whoop. The Texan then grabbed a violin that belonged to Chief Engineer Lieutenant Robert Mars, jumped overboard, and swam to the bank. When he got up on the bank, he mounted a caisson and began playing and dancing to the tune of "Dixie." Then his comrades, overwhelmed with their accomplishment, paddled out in sugar coolers and swarmed aboard the gunboat to celebrate. It was indeed a happy time for a courageous unit.[41]

---

[41] References: Morris Raphael's *A Gunboat Named Diana;* Morris Raphael's *The Battle in the Bayou Country;* Sergeant H.N. Connor's Diary; J. P. Moore's *History of the 152nd Massachusetts.*

THE REBELS' BRAVE STAND

On April 14th, 1863, the Battle of Irish Bend got into full swing after approximately 8,000 Yankees, who had landed north of Franklin, began attacking Gen. Richard Taylor's forces of around 1,800 men who were "dug-in" around a sugarcane field and along a wooded area. The Rebel Gunboat Diana, which was poised near Bayou Teche, was also ready for action.

A hot exchange of gunfire erupted, causing the Yankee units to lie down in the furrows and ditches seeking cover as best they could. Major Thomas McManus of the 25th Connecticut reported that the Rebels were armed with the smooth bores where every cartridge was charged with a bullet and three buck shots, while his regiment was armed with Enfield rifles. He inferred that each Rebel shot that was fired produced in reality four bullets, which were showered upon his men as compared to a single bullet from each Yankee rifle shot. Shells from the Diana also raked the battlefield, and hand to hand fighting was reported.

McManus stated, "Another roar, a crack, an iron shower, and we see to our dismay, two brazen guns admirably served, trained directly upon us pouring shell grape and canister into our ranks, while their musketry fire grew hotter and fiercer than ever. Our men were nearing the end of their supply of ammunition. If the Confederates had charged upon us they would have annihilated our brigade."

While the Yankee units retreated and were garnering reinforcements, Taylor wisely ordered his small army, which included units from the Bisland front, to fall back and make their exodus by the Harding cut-off road—they completely evaded the Union juggernaut.[42]

---

[42] Morris Raphael's *The Battle in the Bayou Country* and also his *A Gunboat Named Diana*; James Hosmer's *The Color Guard*; Homer Sprague's *History of the 13th Connecticut*; Henry Goodell's *25th Connecticut Volunteers*.

INDEX

ABOUT MORRIS RAPHAEL

Morris Raphael, a resident of New Iberia, Louisiana, and native of Natchez, Mississippi, has lived in Acadiana for over six decades. He is a retired project engineer who has a firm background in journalism.

Raphael is past president of the Attakapas Historical Association, the Iberia Cultural Resources Association, the New Iberia Kiwanis Club, and the Jeanerette Rotary Club. He served on the Council of the Shadows-on-the-Teche at New Iberia, and has served on the board of the St. Mary Chapter of Louisiana Landmarks. He has been a longtime member of the Louisiana Writers Guild, the Louisiana Historical Association, and the National Trust for Historic Preservation.

Raphael has published in many magazines and newspapers and has received several literary awards. He was city editor of *The Franklin Banner-Tribune*, and is the author of 14 books and writes a Sunday column for *The Daily Iberian*. In recognition for his historical works, the United Daughters of the Confederacy honored him with the Jefferson Davis award in 1979. In 1985, he was inducted into the Iberia Parish Second Wind Hall of Fame. For his efforts in advancing Cajun culture Raphael received the Cajun Culture Award in 1991.